# 微波爐食譜 第二集
# Microwave Cooking
## Chinese Style II

發行人：林麗華
編著者：財團法人味全文化教育基金會
翻　譯：史嘉琳
攝　影：江文榮
Publisher：Lee Hwa Lin
Editor：Wei-Chuan Cultural Educational Foundation
English Translation：Karen Steffen Chung
Photography：Williams Chiang
© Copyright 1989, Wei-Chuan Cultural Educational
　Foundation

# 序

　　味全文化教育基金會於民國七十七年出版第一本微波爐食譜,深受大眾喜愛,很多讀者都希望我們能提供更多相關資訊,經過味全家政班老師們一年來的努力, 我們再推出 76 道食譜 ,並且更詳盡的介紹使用微波爐烹飪菜餚的秘訣。

　　對現代人來說,微波爐不再是奢侈品,但是知道如何善用它,並將它的功能發揮的淋漓盡致的人並不多,其實如果買到適當的微波爐使之物盡其用,烹調出來的味道和在爐子上炒的一樣鮮美。例如要爆香蔥或蒜,可先將油在微波爐內預熱二分鐘,放入蔥或蒜再加熱,爆出來的效果和在瓦斯爐上炒的不相上下。

　　當家裡請客或者夫婦兩人都是上班族時,為了節省烹調時間,可以同時使用微波爐及瓦斯爐,以便在最短時間內做出豐富的一餐。例如,當天的晚餐為三菜一湯,可以在微波爐內煮湯及蒸魚,同時在瓦斯爐上炒青菜及炒肉片,這樣不到二十分鐘,一頓香噴噴的菜立即可上桌了。

　　以上只是簡單的舉例,關於「微波爐的秘密」、「微波爐的功能」、「微波爐烹飪用具及其保養方法」,可參考本會所出的第一本微波爐食譜,同時也希望這本書能充份發揮幫助讀者享受微波爐烹調食物的樂趣。

# Preface

Reader response to the Wei-Chuan Cultural Educational Foundation's first book on Chinese-style microwave cooking, published in 1988, has been overwhelmingly positive, and the foundation has received numerous requests for more information on microwave cooking. Thanks to a year of untiring efforts by the teachers of Wei-Chuan's cooking classes, we are now able to present to you recipes for 76 more mouthwatering microwave treats, along with further secrets of successful microwave cooking.

The microwave oven has gone from being a luxury item to a standard home appliance. But how many people really know how to get the most out of their microwave? And how many realize that, it done properly, Chinese food cooked in a microwave can come out just as tempting and tasty as anything made with a regular gas or electric range? Probably not that many.

For example, a first step to many stir-fry dishes made on a regular range is to flavor the oil by frying some green onion or garlic in it. This step can be done with a microwave by preheating the oil for two minutes, then adding the green onion or garlic, and heating again briefly in the microwave. The results are every bit as good with a microwave as with a wok over a gas flame.

When cooking for guests, or if both husband and wife work full-time, a microwave can be used in combination with a conventional range to cut the time spent preparing a meal to a bare minimum. For example, for a traditional Chinese meal of three main dishes and a soup, the microwave can be used to cook the soup and steam a fish while a vegetable and a meat dish are being stir-fried on a conventional range. In this way, a complete, four-course meal can be on the table within 20 minutes.

This, of course, is only a simple example. For more information on the secrets of microwave cooking, the functions of a microwave oven, and utensils and utensil care for microwave cooking, please see the Weichuan Cultural and Educational Foundation's first book on microwave cooking. It is our hope that this second volume of Microwave Cooking, Chinese Style will help you to more fully enjoy and get the most out of your microwave.

*Lee Hwa Lin*

# 本書使用秘訣

● 本書使用700瓦電力的微波爐烹調食物，不同電力的微波爐，烹調時間請彈性調整（大於700瓦宜縮短加熱時間，小於700瓦延長加熱時間）。

● A 700W microwave oven was used in developing the recipes for this book. If you are using a different size microwave, you may have to adjust the cooking time accordingly (for microwaves larger than 700W, reduce cooking time; for microwaves smaller than 700W, increase cooking time as necessary).

● 本書所示範的烹調步驟，沒特別說明加蓋（或加保鮮膜），就表示不必加蓋。沒指明以多少電力加熱，就表示以各廠牌的最高電力加熱。

● Whenever no specific instructions are given to cover the cooking dish (either with a lid or plastic wrap), this means it is to be heated uncovered. Whenever no mention is made of how much power to use, heat at full power.

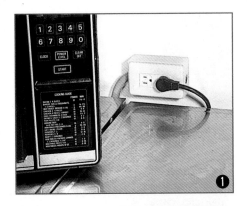

微波爐盡量勿與其他電器共同使用同一插座，以免受到干擾。選購微波爐時要注意500W適合再熱，600W及700W較適合烹調。本書所提供之食譜均以700W微波爐示範。

Avoid plugging other appliances into the outlet used to supply power to your microwave, to prevent interference. When purchasing a microwave, keep in mind that a 500W microwave is best for reheating cooked food, and 600W and 700W microwaves are better suited to cooking from scratch. The recipes in this book were developed with a 700W microwave oven.

放置微波爐的位置宜在左右兩邊及後面留約10公分的距離以散熱。

Keep free a distance of at least 10cm (4″) behind and on each side of the microwave oven, to aid in heat dispersion.

# Microwave Cooking Hints

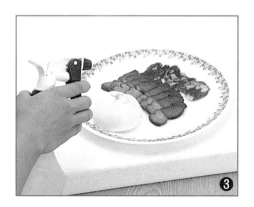

熱包子時先灑上水，以免表面乾燥，臘肉、香腸先切好再灑上少許水份可避免過熱。

Sprinkle a little water on flour-based steamed dumplings and rolls before reheating in the microwave, to prevent drying. Sprinkle a little water over air-dried meat or sausage before heating in the microwave, to prevent them from becoming too hard.

煮湯時勿超過容器的八分滿，以免加熱中湯汁溢出。

When cooking soup, do not fill the bowl more than 80% full, to prevent boiling over.

綜合調味料儘可能事先拌勻，再加入菜餚，味道較易均勻。

Mix seasonings and sauces thoroughly before adding to the dish.

微波爐內若有湯汁溢出時，可以濕布擦乾淨，若味道過重時，可以檸檬汁或白醋加上½杯水加熱4分鐘即可去除異味。

If a dish boils over, wipe up the spill with a damp cloth. If the spill gives off a strong odor, heat some lemon juice or vinegar in 1/2 cup water for 4 minutes in the microwave to deodorize.

# 本書使用秘訣

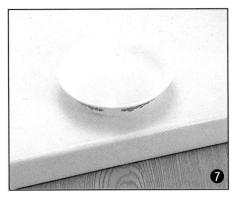

烹調青菜時應先將油加熱後，再與青菜拌勻，作出來的青菜較不會有菁味，且作好之後應立即取出較不易變黃。

When stir-frying vegetables, first preheat the oil, then stir in the vegetables; this prevents the vegetables from having a raw, green taste. Remove the stir-fried vegetables immediately after cooking to retard discoloration.

湯汁較多的菜，以沸水取代冷水可節省時間；加蓋或覆以耐熱膜不可過密，必需留下少許縫或以牙籤戳洞散熱。

For dishes with a large amount of liquid, use boiling water instead of cold water to reduce cooking time. When cooking food covered with a lid or with heat-resistant plastic wrap, be sure to leave the lid open a crack, or to pierce the plastic wrap several times with a toothpick before heating, to allow the hot steam to escape.

爆香時如遇有醬類或水份較少的調味料，加熱時間宜短，約 1 ～ 2 分鐘(視份量決定)才不致燒焦。

If thick sauces or seasonings with a low moisture content are used when frying green onion, garlic, or other condiments to flavor the oil, keep the cooking time short, from 1 to 2 minutes (depending on the amount of food being heated), to prevent scorching.

外層有膜之食品(如雞蛋、香腸等)，加熱前應先用牙籤戳洞，以免加熱後爆破。

When heating foods that are covered with a membrane, such as sausage or eggs, prick several times with a toothpick before heating, to prevent the food from exploding onto the interior of the oven.

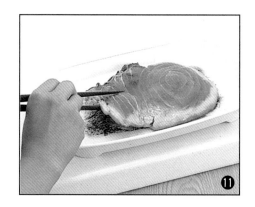

利用微波爐烘烤時，必須用香酥烤盤先預熱後，再將肉、魚放入烤，一面呈金黃色時再翻另一面烤。

When roasting or broiling, first preheat the browning dish, then place the meat or fish on it. Heat until one side of the meat or fish is golden brown, then turn over and heat until the other side is golden brown.

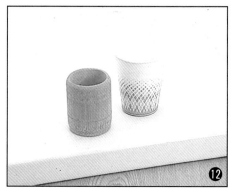

紙製品、竹製品只適合短時間加熱使用。

Food in paper or bamboo containers should be heated for only short periods in the microwave.

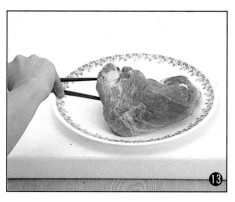

解凍時，可在中途將食物翻面，較快達到解凍效果。

When defrosting frozen food in the microwave, turn the food over about halfway through the heating time, for faster results.

加熱好之菜餚，欲掀開蓋子或耐熱膜時，應朝身體逆向掀起，以防手部被蒸氣燙傷。

When removing the cover or plastic wrap from heated food, be sure to open up the side away from you first, to prevent burning your hand on the hot steam.

# 目錄 Contents

## 粉蒸排骨

材料：

| | | | |
|---|---|---|---|
| 小排骨 | 300公克 | | |
| 蕃薯 | 100公克 | | |
| 葱末 | 1大匙 | | |
| 蒸肉粉 | 1包 | | |

| | |
|---|---|
| 水 | 5大匙 |
| 醬油、甜麵醬、酒 | 各1大匙 |
| 辣豆瓣醬、糖 | 各1大匙 |
| 薑末、蒜末 | 各1大匙 |
| 塩 | ½小匙 |
| 味精、胡椒粉 | 各少許 |

① （包含右列調味料）

❶小排骨洗淨切塊，入①料醃30分鐘後，再入蒸肉粉（圖1）拌勻備用。

❷蕃薯切與排骨同等大小備用。

❸取一中碗先鋪入地瓜（圖2），再將排骨排在上面（圖3），蓋上保鮮膜加熱20分鐘取出，食前灑上葱末即可。

■若使用蒸籠需先泡水20分鐘再使用，蒸籠內先置一盤子，再將地瓜、排骨放入。

## Spiced Steamed Pork Ribs

INGREDIENTS:

| | |
|---|---|
| 300g (⅔ lb.) | pork ribs |
| 100g (¼ lb.) | sweet potatoes |
| 1 T. | minced green onion |
| 1 packet | powder for steamed pork ribs |

① 
| | |
|---|---|
| 5 T. | water |
| 1 T. each: | soy sauce, sweet bean paste, rice wine |
| 1 T. | hot bean paste, sugar |
| 1 T each: | minced ginger root, minced green onion |
| ½ t. | salt |
| pinch | pepper |

❶ Wash the pork ribs and cut into chunks. Marinate in ① for 30 minutes. Mix in the powder for steamed pork ribs thoroughly (illus. 1).

❷ Cut the sweet potatoes into chunks about the same size as the cut pork ribs.

❸ Arrange the sweet potatoes on the bottom of a medium bowl (illus. 2), then arrange the pork ribs on top of the sweet potatoes (illus. 3). Cover the bowl with plastic wrap and heat for 20 minutes. Remove the plastic wrap, sprinkle with the minced green onion, and serve.

■ If using a bamboo steamer, soak it in water for 20 minutes beforehand. Place a shallow bowl in the steamer, then the sweet potatoes, and finally the pork ribs.

## 辣子肉丁 / Hot and Spicy Pork

材料：

| | | | |
|---|---|---|---|
| 梅花肉 | 300公克 | 水 | 3大匙 |
| 荸薺 | 8個 | 醬油 | 2大匙 |
| 油 | 2大匙 | 酒、太白粉 各1大匙 | |
| 葱末 | 1大匙 | ② 糖 | 2小匙 |
| ① 薑末 | 2大匙 | 醋、麻油 各1小匙 | |
| 蒜末 | 1½大匙 | 味精 | ¼小匙 |
| 辣豆瓣醬 | 1大匙 | 胡椒粉 | ⅛小匙 |

❶梅花肉洗淨切半公分小方塊（圖１），入②料醃20分鐘（圖２）備用。荸薺洗淨，每個切成四份（圖３），備用。

❷油２大匙預熱３分鐘，隨入①料爆香１分30秒再與醃過的梅花肉、荸薺丁拌勻，蓋上保鮮膜後入微波爐續熱９分鐘，取出灑上葱末即可。

■請客時可在盤上放置生菜，再將辣子肉丁置中央，較爲美觀。

### INGREDIENTS:

| | | |
|---|---|---|
| | 300g (⅔ lb.) | pork, part fat |
| | 8 | water chestnuts |
| | 2 T. | cooking oil |
| | 1 T. | minced green onion |
| ① | 2 T. | minced ginger root |
| | 1½ T. | minced garlic |
| | 1 T. | hot bean paste |
| | 3 T. | water |
| | 2 T. | soy sauce |
| ② | 1 T. each: | rice wine, cornstarch |
| | 2 t. | sugar |
| | 1 t. each: | rice vinegar, sesame oil |
| | ⅛ t. | pepper |

❶ Wash the pork and cut into 0.5cm (½'') cubes (illus. 1). Mix in ② and marinate for 20 minutes (illus. 2).

❷ Peel the water chestnuts (if using fresh), wash, and quarter each one (illus. 3).

❸ Preheat 2 tablespoons oil in a baking dish for 3 minutes. Add ①, and fry for 1 minute and 30 seconds. Add the marinated pork and the quartered water chestnuts, and mix all the ingredients until combined. Cover with plastic wrap and cook in the microwave for 9 minutes. Remove, sprinkle on the minced green onion, and serve.

■ For a more formal dinner, arrange some lettuce on a serving plate, then pour the Hot and Spicy Pork over the center.

# 紅燒蹄膀 — Pork Shoulder in Soy Sauce

## 材料：

蹄膀 1 個…(約1000公克)

① ┌ 沸水…………… 2½杯
　├ 醬油………… 9大匙
　├ 碎冰糖…… 1½大匙
　└ 五香粉………½小匙

② ┌ 葱……………… 2枝
　├ 八角………… 1朵
　└ 花椒粒……… 1小匙

❶①料拌勻後待涼(圖1)備用。

❷蹄膀洗淨，入①料醃隔夜(圖2)後，加②料以全電力煮15分鐘，再以50％電力加熱60分鐘（中途翻面數次以防上層燒焦)(圖3)即可。

■請客時可以 300 公克燙熱之青江菜或綠色蔬菜圍邊。

## Pork Shoulder in Soy Sauce

INGREDIENTS:

| | | |
|---|---|---|
| 1 | | pork shoulder (about 1000g or 2¼ lb.) |
| ① | 2½ c. | boiling water |
| | 9 T. | soy sauce |
| | 1½ T. | crushed rock candy |
| | ½ t. | five-spice powder |
| ② | 2 stalks | green onion |
| | 1 floweret | star anise |
| | 1 t. | Szechwan peppercorns |

❶ Mix ① until well blended and allow to cool (illus. 1).

❷ Wash the pork shoulder, and marinate in ① overnight (illus. 2). Add ② and microwave at full power for 15 minutes. Reduce to 50% power and microwave for 60 minutes (change the position of meat several times during the cooking process to prevent surface scorching; illus. 3). Serve.

■ For a more formal dinner, 300g (¾ lb.) of ching kang tsai or other leafy green may be blanched and arranged around the Pork Shoulder in Soy Sauce as a garnish.

# 梅子排骨 / Pork Ribs with Preserved Plums

## 材料：

| | |
|---|---|
| 小排骨 | 330公克 |
| 葱末 | 2大匙 |
| 油 | 1大匙 |
| ① 薑末、蒜末 | 各1大匙 |

② 
| | |
|---|---|
| 去籽醃漬梅 | 5粒 |
| 水 | 1½杯 |
| 醃漬梅汁、醬油、酒 | 各1大匙 |
| 糖、太白粉 | 各2小匙 |
| 豆瓣醬 | 1小匙 |

❶ 小排骨剁成24塊，置盤加熱3分鐘（圖1），取出洗淨（圖2）瀝乾（以便去除血水），備用。

❷ 油1大匙預熱2分鐘，爆香①料1分30秒，隨入排骨及②料，加蓋後加熱20分鐘，中途翻動二次（圖3），取出灑上葱花即可。

## Pork Ribs with Preserved Plums

**INGREDIENTS:**

| | | |
|---|---|---|
| | 330g (¾ lb.) | pork ribs |
| | 2 T. | minced green onion |
| | 1 T. | cooking oil |
| ① | 1 T. each | minced ginger, minced garlic |
| ② | 5 | pitted preserved Chinese plums |
| | 1½ c. | water |
| | 1 T. each: | water from soaking preserved plums, soy sauce, rice wine |
| | 2 t. each: | sugar, cornstarch |
| | 1 t. | bean paste |

❶ Chop the pork ribs into 24 chunks, place in a baking dish, and heat in the microwave for 3 minutes (illus. 1). Remove from the microwave, wash the ribs, and drain (illus. 2) to remove the bloody liquid.

❷ Preheat 1 tablespoon oil in a baking dish for 2 minutes. Fry ① in the oil for 1 minute and 30 seconds. Add the ribs and ②, cover, and microwave for 20 minutes. Remove twice during the heating process (illus. 3) to turn over the meat. Remove and sprinkle the minced green onion over the top. Serve.

■ When buying pork ribs, ask your butcher to cut them into chunks for you.

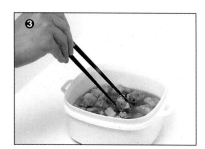

# 鹹蛋蒸肉

## Pork Steamed with Salted Egg

材料：

| | | |
|---|---|---|
| 絞肉…… | 300公克 | |
| 鹹蛋黃……… | 3個 | |

① 鹹蛋白……………… 2個
水…………………… ¼杯
酒、太白粉……各½大匙
蒜末、麻油…… 各1小匙
塩………………… ½小匙
胡椒粉…………… ⅛小匙

❶將鹹蛋黃橫切二半，搓成六個小圓球（圖１）備用。
❷絞肉加上①料順同一方向拌勻（圖２），放入深盤內，上置蛋黃（圖３），蓋上保鮮膜後入微波爐加熱４分鐘即可。
■在國外買不到鹹蛋時，可用以下配方製作。

材料：

雞蛋10個
① 塩………… 1杯
花椒粒… 1大匙
② 水……… 6杯
酒……… 3大匙

❶雞蛋洗淨，瀝乾備用。
❷①料裝入大碗內，入微波爐加熱１分鐘，隨入②料，加蓋續熱３分鐘，取出攪拌一次，再加熱３分鐘至塩全部溶化，取出待涼後，倒入玻璃瓶或甕內，再放入雞蛋，加蓋浸泡30天即可。

### INGREDIENTS:

| | | |
|---|---|---|
| | 300g (⅔ lb.) | ground pork |
| | 3 | salted egg yolks |
| ① | 2 | salted egg whites |
| | ¼ c. | water |
| | ½ T. each: | rice wine, cornstarch |
| | 1 t. each: | minced garlic, sesame oil |
| | ½ t. | salt-pepper |
| | ⅛ t. | pepper |

❶ Halve the cooked salted egg yolks, and shape each half yolk into a little ball (illus. 1).
❷ Mix ① into the ground pork, always stirring in the same direction, until thoroughly blended (illus. 2). Place in a deep dish, and top with the egg yolk balls (illus. 3). Cover with plastic wrap and microwave for 4 minutes. Serve.
■ If salted eggs are unavailable in your area, use the following method to make your own.

### INGREDIENTS:

| | | |
|---|---|---|
| | 10 | chicken eggs |
| ① | 1 c. | salt |
| | 1 T. | Szechwan peppercorns |
| ② | 6 c. | water |
| | 3 T. | rice wine |

❶ Wash and dry the eggs.
❷ Put ① in a large bowl and heat 1 minute in the microwave. Add ②, cover, and heat another 3 minutes. Remove to stir, then heat another 3 minutes in the microwave to completely dissolve the salt. Remove and allow to cool. Pour into a large, clean, wide-mouthed jar, then carefully lower the eggs into the brine. Cover and allow to cure for 30 days. The salted eggs are now ready to use in recipes calling for salted eggs.

# 竹筍燒肉 / Pork with Bamboo Shoots

材料：

| | | | |
|---|---|---|---|
| 五花肉………… 200公克 | | ② 水…………………¾杯 | |
| 筍……2枝（淨重240公克） | | 醬油………… 3大匙 | |
| 油………………… 2大匙 | | 酒………… 1大匙 | |
| ① 蒜……… 3個（拍碎） | | 糖………… 1小匙 | |
| 葱………… 2枝 | | | |

❶筍去皮（圖1）切滾刀塊（圖2），五花肉切0.5×1×3公分塊狀（圖3）備用。

❷油2大匙預熱2分鐘，爆香①料1分30秒後，加入筍塊、五花肉及②料拌勻並醃15分鐘，加蓋入微波爐續熱20分鐘即可。

■一般筍有綠竹筍、麻筍、桂竹筍、孟宗筍等類，可隨季節的不同選用，其中尤以綠竹筍最鮮嫩好吃，如在國外買不到新鮮筍時可以筍罐代之。

## INGREDIENTS:

| | | |
|---|---|---|
| 200g (½ lb.) | | pork belly meat (part lean, part fat) |
| 2 | | fresh bamboo shoots (about 240g or 8½ oz. net weight) |
| 2 T. | | cooking oil |
| ① | 3 cloves | garlic, smashed |
| | 2 stalks | green onion |
| ② | ¾ c. | water |
| | 3 T. | soy sauce |
| | 1 T. | rice wine |
| | 1 t. | sugar |

❶ Husk the bamboo shoots (illus. 1) and roll-cut (illus. 2). Cut the pork belly meat into 0.5×1×3cm (¼'' × ½ × 1¼'') strips (illus. 3).

❷ Preheat 2 tablespoons oil for 2 minutes in the microwave. Fry ① in the oil for 1 minute and 30 seconds. Add the bamboo shoots, the pork, and ②, and mix together well. Let marinate for 15 minutes. Cover and heat for 20 minutes in the microwave. Serve.

■ Any of the many species of bamboo shoots available may be used, depending on what is in season. Green bamboo shoots are the tastiest and most tender. If fresh bamboo shoots are unavailable in your area, canned bamboo shoots may be substituted.

# 梅菜扣肉 / Pork with Chinese Preserved Greens

## 材料：

| | | | | |
|---|---|---|---|---|
| 五花肉 | 450公克 | | 水 | ½杯 |
| 梅乾菜 | 50公克 | | 醬油 | ¼杯 |
| 水 | 1½杯 | ① | 酒 | 1大匙 |
| | | | 糖 | 2小匙 |
| | | | 味精 | ⅛小匙 |

❶梅乾菜洗淨，擠去水份切碎（圖1）備用。

❷五花肉切成3公分長，0.5公分寬之厚片，排在深碗內（圖2），其上置梅乾菜及①料（圖3），醃30分鐘，加蓋後加熱40分鐘（中途每隔10分鐘加½杯水，以防縮乾及上層表面燒焦），即可取出倒扣盤中供食。

■梅乾菜又名覆菜、福菜、濕菜，是將大芥菜經日曬、塩醃，覆於缸中，並將容器倒覆於地上，使其在無水狀態下醃成特有風味的鹹酸菜。

## INGREDIENTS:

| | | |
|---|---|---|
| 450g (1 lb.) | | pork belly meat (part lean, part fat) |
| 50g (1¾ oz.) | | Chinese preserved greens (mei kan tsai) |
| | 1½ c. | water |
| ① | ½ c. | water |
| | ¼ c. | soy sauce |
| | 1 T. | rice wine |
| | 2 t. | sugar |

❶ Wash the Chinese preserved greens, squeeze out the excess moisture, then chop finely (illus. 1).

❷ Cut the pork belly meat into thick 3×0.5cm (1¼'' × ¼'') strips, and arrange in a deep bowl (illus. 2). Arrange the chopped Chinese preserved greens and ① on the pork strips (illus. 3). Marinate for 30 minutes, cover, and heat in the microwave for 40 minutes (add ½ cup water every 10 minutes to prevent drying out and the top surface from burning). Invert the bowl over a serving dish to remove the contents, and serve.

■ Chinese preserved greens are made by drying Chinese mustard greens in the sun, and curing them with salt in a clay pot. The pot is inverted on the ground to keep moisture out and allow the greens to develop a distinctive tart-salty flavor.

## 回鍋肉

## Twice-Cooked Pork

材料：

豬腿肉…………150公克

① {
豆干(切片)…………
………1塊(130公克)
包心菜(切片)………
……¼個(200 公克)
蔥…………… 8段
}

② {
油…………… 2大匙
辣豆瓣醬…… 1大匙
醬油………… 1大匙
甜麵醬……… 1小匙
酒……………½ 大匙
糖……………½ 小匙
塩……………⅛ 小匙
}

❶ 豬腿肉洗淨，置盤加蓋加熱 4 分鐘，取出待涼切薄
片(圖 1)備用。

❷ ②料入微波爐加熱 2 分鐘，入①料、豬腿肉片並拌勻
(圖 2)，續熱 5 分鐘即可。

INGREDIENTS:

150g (⅓ lb.)      pork (shank)

① {
1 cake     pressed bean curd, sliced
(130g or ¼ lb.)
¼     cabbage, sliced
(200g or 7 oz.)
8 sections     green onion
}

② {
2 T.     cooking oil
1 T.     hot bean paste
1 T.     soy sauce
1 t.     sweet bean paste
½ T.     rice wine
½ t.     sugar
⅛ t.     salt
}

❶ Wash the pork, place in an oven dish,
cover, and heat 4 minutes. Remove, allow
to cool, and cut into thin slices (illus. 1).

❷ Heat ② in the microwave for 2 minutes.
Add ① and the sliced pork and mix well
(illus. 2). Heat 5 minutes and serve.

6人份
**SERVES 6**

## 京醬肉絲

## Peking Style Shredded Pork

材料：

| 里肌肉 | 300公克 |
| 京葱 | 1枝 |

① 
| 水 | 4大匙 |
| 油 | 3大匙 |
| 甜麵醬 | 2大匙 |
| 醬油、酒 | 各1大匙 |
| 糖、太白粉 | |
| | 各²⁄₃大匙 |
| 味精 | ¼小匙 |

❶京葱去頭尾，洗淨切３公分長段，再切成細絲，泡
水片刻後（圖１）瀝乾置盤備用。

❷里肌肉剔除白筋切細絲，入①料醃10分鐘，放入盤
中，蓋上保鮮膜（圖２）後，入微波爐加熱４分鐘，
取出放在京葱絲上，食用時再拌勻即可。

INGREDIENTS:

| 300 g (²⁄₃ lb.) | lean pork |
| 1 stalk | large Chinese green onion |

① 
| 4 T. | water |
| 3 T. | cooking oil |
| 2 T. | sweet bean paste |
| 1 T. each: | soy sauce, rice wine |
| ²⁄₃ t. each: | sugar, cornstarch |

❶ Cut the ends off of the green onion, wash, and
cut into 3cm (1¼″) sections. Cut the sections
lengthwise into shreds.   Soak in water briefly
(illus. 1), drain, and set aside in a dish.

❷ Remove the white sinews and shred the pork.
Marinate in ① for 10 minutes. Place in a dish
and cover with plastic wrap (illus. 2). Heat in
the microwave for 4 minutes. Remove and
pour the pork shreds   onto the plate with the
shredded green onion. Mix together well
before eating.

■ If large Chinese green onion is unavailable,
substitute 10 regular green onions (scallions),
using only the white portion.

6人份
**SERVES 6**

## 豉汁排骨

## Pork Ribs in Black Bean Sauce

材料：

| | | | | |
|---|---|---|---|---|
| 小排骨 | 375公克 | | 醬油 | 3大匙 |
| ① | 豆豉 | 1½大匙 | ② | 太白粉 | 1½小匙 |
| | 葱末 | 1大匙 | | 酒 | 1大匙 |
| | 蒜、薑末 | 各⅔大匙 | | 糖 | ½大匙 |
| | 紅辣椒 | 1條 | | 麻油 | ½小匙 |
| 葱花 | 1枝 | | | |

❶小排骨剁約1.5公分立方塊，入①料及②料（圖1）拌匀，至少醃30分鐘，再加蓋加熱10分鐘，取出灑上葱花（圖2）即可。

INGREDIENTS:

| | | |
|---|---|---|
| 375g (¾ lb.) | | pork ribs |
| ① | 1½ T. | fermented black beans |
| | 1 T. | minced green onion |
| | ⅔ T. each: | minced garlic, minced ginger root |
| | 1 | small red chili pepper |
| 1 stalk | | green onion, chopped |
| ② | 3 T. | soy sauce |
| | 1½ t. | cornstarch |
| | 1 T. | rice wine |
| | ½ T. | sugar |
| | ½ t. | sesame oil |

❶ Cut the pork ribs into 1.5cm (⅝") cubes. Add ① and ② (illus. 1), mix well, and marinate at least 30 minutes. Cover and heat 10 minutes. Remove, sprinkle on chopped green onion (illus. 2), and serve.

6人份
**SERVES 6**

## 蘿蔔綉球

## Microwave Meatballs

材料：

| 絞肉 | 300公克 |
| 胡蘿蔔絲 | 90公克 |
| 葱末 | 1大匙 |
| 薑末 | ½小匙 |

① | 水 | 3大匙 |
| 醬油、麻油 | 各1大匙 |
| 太白粉 | 1大匙 |
| 糖 | ½小匙 |
| 胡椒粉 | ½小匙 |
| 塩 | ¼小匙 |

② | 開水 | ½杯 |
| 塩、味精 | 各¼小匙 |

③ | 水 | 1大匙 |
| 太白粉 | ½大匙 |

❶絞肉、胡蘿蔔絲、葱末、薑末及①料拌勻後（圖1）
，攪拌至有黏性，作成12個丸子（圖2），入②料加
熱7分鐘取出。

❷將湯汁瀝出，入③料加熱30秒勾芡淋在丸子上即成
。

INGREDIENTS:

| 300g (⅔ lb.) | ground pork |
| 90g (3 oz.) | shredded carrot |
| 1 T. | minced green onion |
| ½ t. | minced ginger root |

① | 3 T. | water |
| 1 T. each: | soy sauce, sesame oil, cornstarch |
| ½ t. each: | sugar, pepper |
| ¼ t. | salt |

② | ½ c. | water |
| ¼ t. | salt |

③ | 1 T. | water |
| ½ T. | cornstarch |

❶ Mix the ground pork, shredded carrot, minced green onion, minced ginger root, and ① until well combined (illus. 1). Continue to mix until the mixture becomes sticky. Form into 12 balls (illus. 2). Add ② and heat 7 minutes. Remove.

❷ Drain off the liquid, add ③ , and heat 30 seconds to thicken. Pour over the meatballs and serve.

6人份
**SERVES 6**

# 香菇燒肉     Pork With Mushrooms

## 材料

| | | | |
|---|---|---|---|
| 夾心豬肉·········300公克 | | 八角··············1個 | |
| 竹筍片············80公克 | ② | 花椒··············¼匙 | |
| 香菇5朵···········25公克 | | 水···············1½杯 | |
| ① 醬油········2½大匙 | | 醬油·············4大匙 | |
| 糖···········¼小匙 | ③ | 酒··············1大匙 | |
| 胡椒粉··········少許 | | 糖··············½大匙 | |
| | | 塩·············¼小匙 | |

❶香菇泡軟去蒂備用。

❷豬肉切片，加熱30分鐘以去血水，取出洗淨瀝乾(圖1)，入①料醃15分鐘。

❸②料加熱３分鐘爆香，續入③料、竹筍、香菇及醃好之豬肉片(圖２)，續熱15分鐘即可。

## Pork With Mushrooms

INGREDIENTS:

| | | |
|---|---|---|
| 300g (⅔ lb.) | | pork (part fat, part lean) |
| 80g (3 oz.) | | bamboo shoots |
| 5 | | dried Chinese black mushrooms (25g or 1 oz.) |
| ① | 2½ T. | soy sauce |
| | ¼ t. | sugar |
| | pinch | pepper |
| ② | 1 floweret | star anise |
| | ¼ t. | Szechwan peppercorns |
| | 1½ c. | water |
| ③ | 4 T. | soy sauce |
| | 1 T. | rice wine |
| | ½ T. | sugar |
| | ¼ t. | salt |

❶ Soak the mushrooms until soft and remove the stems.

❷ Slice the pork. Heat 3 minutes to remove the bloody liquid. Remove, rinse clean, and drain (illus. 1). Add ① and marinate 15 minutes.

❸ Heat ② for 3 minutes. Add ③ , the bamboo shoots, mushrooms, and marinated sliced pork (illus. 2). Heat 15 minutes and serve.

6人份
**SERVES 6**

# 東瀛雞丁

# Chicken Nippon

材料：

| | | |
|---|---|---|
| 雞胸肉（淨肉）‥‥260公克 | | 水‥‥‥‥‥ 2大匙 |
| 青椒（切小塊）‥‥‥90公克 | | 油‥‥‥‥ 1½大匙 |
| 紅辣椒（切小塊）‥‥10公克 | | 味噌‥‥‥‥ 1大匙 |
| 蒜片‥‥‥‥‥‥‥10公克 | ① | 太白粉‥‥‥‥ 1大匙 |
| 油‥‥‥‥‥‥‥ 2大匙 | | 醬油‥‥‥‥‥ 2大匙 |
| | | 酒、糖‥‥‥各½小匙 |
| | | 麻油‥‥‥‥‥½小匙 |
| | | 塩‥‥‥‥‥‥¼小匙 |

❶ 雞胸肉拍鬆切丁，入①料醃約20分鐘。

❷ 油 2 大匙，加蒜片爆香 2 分鐘，入青椒、紅辣椒（圖1）續熱 1 分30秒，取出備用。

❸ 醃好的雞肉加熱 3 分30秒取出，拌入爆香後之青椒、紅辣椒（圖2）續熱 1 分鐘即可。

INGREDIENTS:

| | |
|---|---|
| 260g (9 oz.) | chicken breast fillet |
| 90g (3 oz.) | green pepper, cut in small pieces |
| 10g (⅓ oz.) | red chili pepper, cut in small pieces |
| 10g (⅓ oz.) | sliced fresh garlic |
| 2 T. | cooking oil |

| | | |
|---|---|---|
| | 2 T. | water |
| | 1½ T. | cooking oil |
| ① | 1 T. each: | miso, cornstarch |
| | 2 T. | soy sauce |
| | ½ t. each: | rice wine, sugar, sesame oil |
| | ¼ t. | salt |

❶ Tenderize the chicken breast fillet by striking with the dull edge of a cleaver, then cube. Mix in ① and marinate 20 minutes.

❷ Heat the sliced garlic in 2 tablespoons oil for 2 minutes. Add the green pepper and red chili pepper (illus. 1) and heat another 1 minute, 30 seconds. Remove.

❸ Heat the marinated chicken for 3 minutes, 30 seconds and remove. Add the fried green pepper and red chili pepper (illus. 2). Heat another minute and serve.

6人份
**SERVES 6**

# 臘腸香菇雞

## Steamed Chicken With Sausage

材料：

| | |
|---|---|
| 雞腿2隻⋯⋯⋯(540公克) | 醬油⋯⋯⋯⋯½大匙 |
| 廣式臘腸⋯⋯⋯(50公克) | 麻油、酒⋯各½大匙 |
| 葱段⋯⋯⋯⋯⋯20公克 ① | 太白粉、油各½大匙 |
| 香菇⋯⋯⋯⋯⋯5公克 | 糖⋯⋯⋯⋯⋯½小匙 |
| 薑片⋯⋯⋯⋯⋯5公克 | 塩、胡椒粉各¼小匙 |

❶香菇泡軟去蒂，臘腸切片，雞腿剁塊均入①料、葱段、薑片拌勻醃15分鐘。

❷取扣碗，香菇置底部，邊緣以臘腸裝飾（圖1），將雞肉排滿後（圖2），加蓋加熱10分鐘後倒扣於盤子上即可。

■各家所製臘腸風味不同，宜選味甘芳香者。

INGREDIENTS:

| | |
|---|---|
| 2 | chicken legs (540g or 1¼ lb.) |
| 50g (1¾ oz.) | Cantonese-style sausage |
| 20g (¾ oz.) | green onion, cut in sections |
| 5g (⅙ oz.) | dried Chinese black mushrooms |
| 5g (⅙ oz.) | sliced ginger root |
| ① ½ T. each: | soy sauce, sesame oil, rice wine, cornstarch, cooking oil |
| ½ t. | sugar |
| ¼ t. each: | salt, pepper |

❶ Soak the black mushrooms until soft and remove the stems. Slice the Cantonese-style sausage. Chop the chicken legs into pieces. Place the chicken in a bowl and add ① , the green onion sections, and the sliced ginger root. Mix well and leave undisturbed 15 minutes.

❷ Arrange the mushrooms in the bottom of a steaming bowl. Place the sausage slices around the mushrooms in a decorative pattern (illus. 1). Last add the chicken leg pieces (illus. 2). Cover and heat 10 minutes. Invert onto a plate and serve.

■ Chinese sausage comes in many different flavors; choose a sweet and fragrant kind for this dish.

6人份
**SERVES 6**

## 竹節雞盅

材料：

| | | | |
|---|---|---|---|
| 雞胸肉············ | 200公克 | 醬油··········· | 1大匙 |
| 荸薺················· | 65公克 | 酒··············· | ½大匙 |
| 肥肉················· | 60公克 | ① 太白粉········ | 1小匙 |
| 熱水··············· | 1½杯 | 塩··············· | ½小匙 |
| 竹節··············· | 6節 | 味精··········· | ¼小匙 |

❶ 雞胸肉與肥肉均剁成泥，荸薺磨成泥後與雞肉、肥肉泥及①料（圖1）拌勻，再甩打使有彈性，並徐徐加入熱水（圖2）拌勻，將這些材料倒入每個竹節中（約8分滿）。

❷ 將竹節置盤子中，上覆耐熱膜，加熱6分鐘即可。

6人份
**SERVES 6**

# Chicken-in-Bamboo

INGREDIENTS:

| | | |
|---|---|---|
| 200g (7 oz.) | | chicken breast fillet |
| 65g (2¼ oz.) | | water chestnuts |
| 60g (2 oz.) | | fat pork |
| 1½ c. | | hot water |
| 6 | | bamboo-section cups |
| ① | 1 T. | soy sauce |
| | ½ T. | rice wine |
| | 1 t. | cornstarch |
| | ½ t. | salt |

❶ Chop the chicken breast meat and fat pork into a paste. Grind the water chestnuts into a puree and mix with ① into the chicken-pork paste (illus. 1) until smooth. Throw the paste against a cutting board several times to make it springier. Slowly add the hot water to the paste (illus. 2) and mix until smooth.

❷ Pour the mixture into each of the bamboo-section cups until about ⅘ full.

❸ Place the bamboo-section cups on a plate, and cover with heat-resistant plastic wrap. Heat 6 minutes and serve.

# 香菇蒸雞

## Chicken Steamed with Black Mushrooms

材料：

| | | | |
|---|---|---|---|
| 雞 | 600公克 | 水 | ¾杯 |
| 香菇 | 6朵 | 酒 | 1大匙 |
| 木耳 | 40公克 ① | 醬油 | 1½小匙 |
| | | 塩、糖 | 各½小匙 |
| | | 味精 | ⅛小匙 |
| | ② | 太白粉、水 | 各1½小匙 |

❶香菇泡軟去蒂，木耳洗淨切小塊，雞洗淨剁小塊均備用。

❷取一深碗，先將香菇排在碗底（圖1），上置雞塊（圖2），最後入木耳及①料（圖3），醃約半小時，加蓋後加熱12分鐘，取出並將蒸汁倒在碗內，其他材料倒扣盤中備用。

❸蒸汁加②料勾芡加熱30秒，淋在香菇蒸雞上即可。

INGREDIENTS:

| | | |
|---|---|---|
| 600g (1⅓ lb.) | | chicken |
| 6 | | dried Chinese black mushrooms |
| 40g (1⅓ oz.) | | wood ears (tree fungus) |
| ① | ¾ c. | water |
| | 1 T. | cooking wine |
| | 1½ t. | soy sauce |
| | ½ t. each: | salt, sugar |
| ② | 1½ t. each: | cornstarch, water |

❶ Soak the dried Chinese black mushrooms until soft, remove the tough stems, and set aside. Wash the wood ears (and soak until soft, if using dried wood ears), then cut into small pieces. Set aside. Wash the chicken and chop into chunks. Set aside.

❷ Arrange the Chinese black mushrooms over the bottom of a deep bowl (illus. 1). Place the chicken pieces on top (illus. 2), then top with the wood ears and ① (illus. 3). Marinate about 30 minutes. Cover and heat in the microwave 12 minutes. Pour off the liquid into a bowl, then invert the other ingredients onto a plate and set aside.

❸ Add ② to the poured off liquid and heat 30 seconds in the microwave to thicken. Drizzle over the Chicken Steamed with Black Mushrooms and serve.

# 洋葱雞      Chicken with Onions

材料：

| | | | |
|---|---|---|---|
| 雞腿……2隻（約600公克） | | 水……………………½杯 | |
| 洋葱絲…………300公克 | | 醬油…………½大匙 | |
| 榨菜末…………70公克 | ① | 酒、糖……各1小匙 | |
| 油……………………3大匙 | | 塩…………………½小匙 | |
| 醬油………………1大匙 | | 薑…………………3片 | |
| | ② | 水…………………1大匙 | |
| | | 太白粉………1小匙 | |

❶油2大匙、洋葱絲、榨菜末及①料拌勻備用。

❷雞腿內側用刀劃開（圖1），以醬油1大匙抹勻（圖2），醃約20分鐘後，淋上1大匙油，蓋上保鮮膜後加熱5分鐘取出，拆開保鮮膜，置❶料於雞腿上（圖3），加蓋續熱15分鐘。

❸食前取出洋葱鋪底，雞腿切塊，置於洋葱上，餘汁以②料勾芡加熱30秒，淋於雞腿上即可。

## INGREDIENTS:

| | | |
|---|---|---|
| 2 | | chicken legs (600g or 1⅓ lb.) |
| 300g (⅔ lb.) | | onion, cut into half-rings |
| 70g (2½ oz.) | | Szechwan pickled mustard greens, minced |
| 3 T. | | cooking oil |
| 1 T. | | soy sauce |
| ① | ½ c. | water |
| | ½ T. | soy sauce |
| | 1 t. each: | rice wine, sugar |
| | ½ t. | salt |
| | 3 slices | ginger root |
| ② | 1 T. | water |
| | 1 t. | cornstarch |

❶ Mix 2 tablespoons oil, the onion half-rings, the minced Szechwan pickled mustard greens, and ① together until well blended.

❷ Score the chicken legs on the inner portion of the joint with the thigh (illus. 1). Rub 1 tablespoon soy sauce into the chicken legs evenly (illus. 2), and marinate for 20 minutes. Spoon 1 tablespoon of cooking oil over the chicken legs. Cover with plastic wrap and heat in the microwave for 5 minutes. Remove the plastic wrap, and top the chicken legs with the ingredients in step ❶ (illus. 3). Cover and heat in the microwave for another 15 minutes.

❸ Before serving, remove the onion and spread over a plate. Chop the chicken legs into chunks, and place on top of the onion. Mix the liquid remaining from the chicken legs with ② until blended. Heat for 30 seconds in the microwave, drizzle over the chicken legs, and serve.

# 花仁雞丁

材料：

| | | |
|---|---|---|
| 雞胸肉··········· 300公克 | | 薑末、葱末、蒜末··· |
| 蒜頭花生··············½杯 | ② | ·············· 各1大匙 |
| 油················ 3大匙 | | 紅辣椒········ 1小匙 |

① ｛ 水············· 5大匙
太白粉····· 1½小匙
酒············· 1小匙
塩、麻油···各½小匙
糖、胡椒粉··········
··········各¼小匙
味精··········⅛小匙 ｝

❶ 雞胸肉拍鬆後切丁（圖1），入①料醃10分鐘備用。
❷ 油3大匙入微波爐預熱3分鐘，再爆香②料1分30
秒，取出與❶料拌勻（圖2），蓋上保鮮膜後加熱5
分鐘取出，拌入蒜頭花生（圖3）即可。
■ 1. 買不到蒜頭花生時，可參考下列方法自製。
材料：
生花生················· 1杯
塩················· ½小匙
①蒜末、油··· 各1大匙
❶生花生置碗中，不加蓋，入微波爐加熱3分鐘
後，趁熱去膜。
❷①料與去膜的花生拌勻，不加蓋續熱5分鐘，
取出，趁熱拌入塩即可。

## INGREDIENTS:

| | | |
|---|---|---|
| 300g (⅔ lb.) | | chicken breast fillets |
| ½ c. | | garlic-flavored peanuts |
| 3 T. | | cooking oil |
| ① | 5 T. | water |
| | 1½ t. | cornstarch |
| | 1 t. | rice wine |
| | ½ t. each: | salt, sesame oil |
| | ¼ t. each: | sugar, pepper |
| ② | 1 T. each: | minced ginger root, minced green onion, minced garlic |
| | 1 t. | red chili pepper, cut in thin rings |

❶ Pound the chicken breast fillets until tender and cube (illus. 1). Add ① and marinate for 10 minutes.
❷ Add 3 tablespoons cooking oil to a baking dish and preheat in the microwave for 3 minutes. Fry ② in the oil for another 1 minute and 30 seconds. Remove and mix with the chicken until well blended (illus. 2). Cover with plastic wrap and heat for 5 minutes. Remove, stir in the garlic-flavored peanuts (illus. 3), and serve.
■ If garlic-flavored peanuts are unavailable, make them yourself with the following recipe:

INGREDIENTS:

| | |
|---|---|
| 1 c. | raw peanuts |
| ½ t. | salt |
| ① 1 T. each: | minced garlic, cooking oil |

❶ Heat the peanuts in the microwave for 3 minutes, uncovered. Remove the skins while still hot.
❷ Mix the peanuts with ① until blended. Heat in the microwave another 5 minutes, uncovered. Remove, and mix in the salt while the peanuts are still hot.

# 咖哩雞

# Curried Chicken

材料：

| | | | |
|---|---|---|---|
| 雞腿 | 600公克 | | |
| 洋葱、馬鈴薯、胡蘿蔔 | | 水 | 2杯 |
| | 150公克 | ② 番茄醬 | 2大匙 |
| 油 | 2大匙 | 塩 | 1½小匙 |
| ① 麵粉 | 3大匙 | 糖 | ½小匙 |
| 咖哩粉 | 2大匙 | | |

❶雞腿洗淨剁成3×4公分小塊備用。
❷馬鈴薯、胡蘿蔔去皮洗淨，切1公分正方塊備用，洋葱也切1×1公分小塊備用。
❸油2大匙預熱2分鐘（圖1），再爆香洋葱2分鐘（圖2），取出與①料拌勻後再入馬鈴薯、胡蘿蔔及②料，加蓋熱10分鐘，再放入雞塊續熱15分鐘即可。

INGREDIENTS:

| | | |
|---|---|---|
| 600g (1⅓ lb.) | | chicken legs |
| 150g (⅓ lb.) each: | | onion, potato, carrot |
| 2 T. | | cooking oil |
| ① | 3 T. | flour |
| | 2 T. | curry powder |
| ② | 2 c. | water |
| | 2 T. | ketchup |
| | 1½ t. | salt |
| | ½ t. | sugar |

❶ Wash the chicken legs and chop into 3×4cm (1¼″×1½″) chunks.
❷ Peel and wash the potato, carrot, and onion. Cut into 1 cm (½″) cubes.
❸ Preheat 2 tablespoons oil in the microwave for 2 minutes (illus. 1), then fry the onion in the oil for 2 minutes (illus. 2). Remove and mix in ①, then stir in the potato, carrot, and ②. Cover and heat in the microwave for 10 minutes. Finally, stir in the chicken and heat for another 15 minutes. Serve.

6 人份
**SERVES 6**

# 雞絲拉皮

# Chicken With Bean Sheet

材料：

| | | | | |
|---|---|---|---|---|
| 雞胸肉 | 140公克 | | 醬油、高湯各 2 大匙 | |
| 粉皮 | 135公克 | | 芝麻醬 | 1½大匙 |
| 小黃瓜 | 150公克 | | 花生醬 | 1½大匙 |
| 熱水 | 1 杯 | ② | 醋、葱末 | 各 1 大匙 |
| ① | 酒 | ¼小匙 | | 糖、蒜末 | 各 1 小匙 |
| | 塩、太白粉各⅛小匙 | | 薑末 | 1小匙 |
| | | | 塩 | ¼小匙 |

❶ 雞胸肉入①料醃10分鐘，加熱 4 分鐘取出待涼，逆紋切細絲備用。

❷ 粉皮切寬約 1 公分之長條，加熱水 1 杯，加熱 3 分鐘，取出漂涼備用；小黃瓜切細絲，加塩¼小匙，醃片刻以去生味，備用。

❸ 粉皮置盤底上加小黃瓜（圖 1），再放雞胸肉絲（圖 2），食時淋上調好之②料，即可。

INGREDIENTS:

| | | |
|---|---|---|
| 140g (5 oz.) | | chicken breast meat |
| 135g (4¾ oz.) | | dried mung bean sheet |
| 150g (⅓ lb.) | | gherkin cucumbers |
| 1 c. | | hot water |
| ① | ¼ t. | rice wine |
| | ⅛ t. each: | salt, cornstarch |
| ② | 2 T. each: | soy sauce, stock |
| | 1½ T. each: | sesame paste, creamy peanut butter |
| | 1 T. each: | rice vinegar, minced green onion |
| | 1 t. each: | sugar, minced garlic, minced ginger root |
| ¼ t. | | salt |

❶ Add ① to the chicken breast meat and marinate 10 minutes. Heat 4 minutes, remove, and allow to cool. Cut against the grain into shreds.

❷ Soak the mung bean sheet until soft. Cut into strips about 1 cm (⅓″) wide. Add 1 cup hot water and heat 3 minutes. Remove and cool in tap water. Shred the gherkin cucumber and add ¼ teaspoon salt. Allow to set a moment to take away the green flavor.

❸ Spread the mung bean strips on a plate and top with the gherkin cucumber shreds (illus. 1). Spread the shredded chicken over the top (illus. 1). When ready to serve, pour ② over the top as a dressing.

## 雞　　凍

# Chicken Aspic

材料：

| 雞腿 2 隻 | ……… | 500公克 |
| 熱水 | …………………… | ½杯 |
| 香菜 | …………………… | 少許 |

① {
水 ……………… 2杯
醬油 ………… 3大匙
酒 …………… 2大匙
葱 ………… 1小匙
薑片 ………… 2片
塩、糖 …… 各½小匙
}

② 胡椒粉、味精各少許

③ {
冷開水 …………½杯
吉利丁 …… 3大匙
}

❶ 雞腿去骨及皮後加熱 1 分鐘以去血水，入①料加熱
20分鐘取出，並留下 1½杯雞汁備用；雞肉待涼撕
成絲。

❷ 雞汁1½杯加熱水½杯及②料加熱 1 分30秒後，將油
過濾（圖1），趁熱拌入③料及雞絲拌勻，再入模型
內待涼（圖2），冷藏使之凝固。食時切塊排盤，上
灑少許香菜末即可。

INGREDIENTS:

| 2 | chicken legs (500g or 1 lb, 1½ oz.) |
| ½ c. | hot water |
| small bunch | fresh coriander |

① {
2 c. water
3 T. soy sauce
2 T. rice wine
1 t. minced green onion
2 slices ginger root
½ t. each: salt, sugar
}

② pinch pepper

③ {
½ c. cold water
3 T. unflavored gelatin
}

❶ Remove the bones and skin from the chicken legs
and heat 1 minute to remove bloody liquid. Add ①
and heat another 20 minutes. Remove. Retain 1½
cups of the cooking liquid. Allow the chicken meat
to cool, then shred.

❷ Add ½ cup hot water and ② to the chicken broth and
heat 1 minute, 30 seconds. Skim the oil (illus. 1). While
still hot, mix in ③ and the shredded chicken until well
combined. Pour into a mold and allow to cool (illus.
2). Cool in the refrigerator until firm. Cut in squares
and arrange on a plate. Sprinkle a little chopped
fresh coriander over the top and serve.

6人份
**SERVES 6**

## 雪白雞捲

## Chicken Sandwich Wraps

材料：

| 雞胸肉 | 100公克 | | 太白粉 | ¼小匙 |
|---|---|---|---|---|
| 馬鈴薯 | 90公克 | ① | 塩 | ⅛小匙 |
| 沙拉 | 90公克 | | 味精 | ⅛小匙 |
| 洋葱末 | 40公克 | | 玻璃紙 (10×15公分) 12張 | |
| 吐司 | 6片 | | | |

❶ 雞胸肉略拍鬆，入①料醃10分鐘，加蓋加熱2分30秒，取出待涼切絲，洋葱末加蓋加熱1分鐘取出均備用。

❷ 馬鈴薯去皮切片，加蓋加熱2分鐘取出，搗成泥狀入沙拉、洋葱末、雞絲等拌勻成餡，分成12份備用。

❸ 吐司切去硬邊，每片橫切成對半共十二片，每一小片吐司包入1份餡 (圖1) 並捲成圓筒狀，再以玻璃紙捲好，兩邊捏緊成糖菓狀 (圖2) 加熱1分鐘即可。

INGREDIENTS:

| 100g (3½ oz.) | chicken breast fillet |
|---|---|
| 90g (3 oz.) | potatoes |
| 90g (3 oz.) | mayonnaise |
| 40g (1½ oz.) | minced onion |
| 6 slices | white bread |
| ① ¼ t. | cornstarch |
| ⅛ t. | salt |
| 12 sheets | cellophane (10 x 15cm or 4″ x 6″) |

❶ Tenderize the chicken breast fillet lightly with the dull edge of a cleaver. Add ① and marinate 10 minutes. Cover and heat 2 minutes, 30 seconds. Remove, allow to cool, and shred with a knife. Cover the minced onion and heat 1 minute. Remove.

❷ Peel and slice the potatoes. Cover and heat 2 minutes. Mash until smooth and add the mayonnaise, minced onion, and shredded chicken. Mix well to form a filling. Divide into 12 equal portions.

❸ Trim the crusts off the white bread and cut each slice in half crosswise. Wrap each half slice around one portion of filling (illus. 1) and form into a cylindrical shape. Wrap each in a sheet of cellophane. Twist the ends as though wrapping a piece of taffy (illus. 2). Heat 1 minute and serve.

6人份
**SERVES 6**

# 滾筒牛肉 | Beef Roulades

## 材料：

| | | | | |
|---|---|---|---|---|
| 牛里肌肉……… | 150公克 | | 醬油……… | 1½大匙 |
| 青蒜……………… | 2枝 | | 酒、水…… 各 | 1大匙 |
| 熟筍………… | 37.5公克 | ① | 太白粉…… | 2小匙 |
| 熟胡蘿蔔……… | 17.5公克 | | 味精……… | ½小匙 |
| 香菇……2朵（ 5公克 ） | | | 胡椒粉……… | ¼小匙 |
| 葱白……………… | 6段 | | 水……………… | ⅓杯 |
| | | ② | 醬油、糖…各 | 1大匙 |
| | | | 味精、麻油各 | ¼小匙 |
| | | ③ | 水……………… | ½大匙 |
| | | | 太白粉……… | ½小匙 |

❶牛里肌肉切薄片拍鬆後入①料醃20分鐘。

❷熟筍、熟胡蘿蔔均切約0.7×4公分長段；蒜白切段，蒜尾撕成細長條(圖1)，置盤中加蓋加熱1分鐘後沖涼備用；香菇泡軟切成6條。

❸牛里肌肉片包入葱白、筍、香菇各1條後捲起(圖2)，以蒜尾綁好(圖3)；另胡蘿蔔、筍、蒜白各1條也以蒜尾綁好。

❹將作法❸所有材料置盤中，入②料加蓋加熱2分30秒後，湯汁瀝出以③料勾芡，加熱30秒後淋於牛肉捲上即可。

## INGREDIENTS:

| | | |
|---|---|---|
| 150g (⅓ lb.) | | lean beef |
| 2 stalks | | garlic (similar to green onion) |
| 37.5g (1½ oz.) | | cooked bamboo shoots |
| 17.5g (½ oz.) | | cooked carrot |
| 2 | | dried Chinese black mushrooms (5g or ⅙ oz.) |
| 6 sections | | green onion (white portion only) |
| ① | 1½ T. | soy sauce |
| | 1 T. each: | rice wine, water |
| | 2 t. | cornstarch |
| | ¼ t. | pepper |
| ② | ⅓ c. | water |
| | 1 T. each: | soy sauce, sugar |
| | ¼ t. | sesame oil |
| ③ | ½ T. | water |
| | ½ t. | cornstarch |

❶ Cut the lean beef into 6 thin slices and tenderize lightly. Mix in ① and marinate 20 minutes.

❷ Cut the cooked bamboo shoots and carrot into 4 x 0.7cm (1½'x ¼') strips. Cut the white portion of the garlic into sections, and tear the green portion into long shreds (illus. 1). Place on a plate, cover, and heat 1 minute. Rinse to cool. Soak the mushrooms until soft and cut into 6 strips.

❸ Wrap the beef slices around one section of green onion (white), and one strip each of bamboo shoot and mushroom· Or roll one strip each of bamboo shoot and carrot and a section of garlic (white) onto each beef roll with a shred of garlic (green) (illus. 2,3).

❹ Arrange the beef rolls on a plate and top with ② . Cover and heat 2 minutes, 30 seconds. Pour off the liquid. Add ③ to the liquid and heat 30 seconds to thicken. Pour over the beef rolls and serve.

# 酸菜牛肉 / Pickled Mustard Cabbage and Beef

材料：

| | | | | |
|---|---|---|---|---|
| 牛里肌肉……… | 300公克 | | 水………… | 1大匙 |
| 酸菜心………… | 90公克 | | 太白粉……… | 1小匙 |
| 薑片、紅辣椒… | 各20公克 | ② | 糖………… | ¾小匙 |
| 油……………… | 2大匙 | | 塩、胡椒粉… | |
| | | | ……………… | 各¼小匙 |
| | 水………… | 2大匙 | | 麻油………… | 少許 |
| | 油………… | 1大匙 | | | |
| ① | 酒、醬油… | 各1小匙 | | | |
| | 糖………… | ½小匙 | | | |
| | 味精、胡椒粉… | 少許 | | | |

❶牛肉洗淨切片，入①料醃約15分鐘，紅辣椒去籽切約1½公分長小片，酸菜切與牛肉片同等大小薄片，泡一下水，撈起瀝乾水份備用。

❷油2大匙（圖1）預熱3分鐘，再爆香薑片1分鐘（圖2）拌入醃好之肉片、酸菜片、紅辣椒片及②料（圖3），蓋上保鮮膜後加熱2分鐘即可。

■牛肉須逆紋切片才嫩。

## Pickled Mustard Cabbage and Beef

INGREDIENTS:

| | | |
|---|---|---|
| 300g (⅔ lb.) | | lean beef |
| 90g (3 oz.) | | pickled mustard cabbage |
| 1 T. (20g) each: | | ginger root slices, red chili pepper |
| 2 T. | | cooking oil |
| | 2 T. | water |
| | 1 T. | cooking oil |
| ① | 1 t. each: | rice wine, soy sauce |
| | ½ t. | sugar |
| | pinch | pepper |
| | 1 T. | water |
| | 1 t. | cornstarch |
| ② | ¾ t. | sugar |
| | ¼ t. each: | salt, pepper |
| | dash | sesame oil |

❶ Wash the beef and slice thinly. Marinate in ① about 15 minutes. Remove the seeds from the red chili pepper and cut into 1.5cm (⅝'') pieces. Cut the pickled mustard cabbage into thin slices about the same size as the beef slices. Soak briefly in water. Remove from water, drain, and set aside.

❷ Preheat 2 tablespoons oil for 3 minutes in the microwave (illus. 1), then fry the ginger slices in the oil for 1 minute (illus. 2). Mix in the marinated beef slices, pickled mustard cabbage slices, red chili pepper, and ② (illus. 3). Cover with plastic wrap, heat in the microwave for 2 minutes, and serve.

| | |
|---|---|
| ## 木瓜牛肉 | # Papaya Beef |

材料：

牛肉‥‥‥‥‥‥ 250公克
木瓜（淨重）‥‥‥ 120公克
葱段‥‥‥‥‥‥‥‥ 6段
油‥‥‥‥‥‥‥‥ 2大匙

① {
水‥‥‥‥‥‥ 3大匙
太白粉、酒‥‥‥‥‥
‥‥‥‥‥‥ 各1大匙
塩‥‥‥‥‥‥ ½小匙
胡椒粉‥‥‥‥ ¼小匙
味精‥‥‥‥‥‥少許
}

❶牛肉切細絲，入①料及葱醃約20分鐘備用。
❷木瓜切0.3公分細絲（圖１）備用。
❸將醃好的牛肉取出，葱段（圖２）丟棄，再拌入油及
　木瓜絲置盤中，蓋上保鮮膜，加熱４分30秒即可。
■此道菜選略熟之木瓜即可，不要太熟，以免切細絲
　後糊爛。

INGREDIENTS:

| | |
|---|---|
| 250g (9 oz.) | beef |
| 120g (¼ lb.) | papaya (net weight) |
| 6 1½″ sections | green onion |
| 2 T. | cooking oil |

① {
| 3 T. | water |
| 1 T. each: | cornstarch, rice wine |
| ½ t. | salt |
| ¼ t. | pepper |
}

❶ Shred the beef. Add the green onion and
　① and marinate about 20 minutes. Set
　aside.
❷ Shred the papaya (illus. 1).
❸ Transfer the marinated beef to a baking
　dish, discard the green onion (illus. 2),
　and mix in the oil and shredded papaya
　(illus. 3). Cover with plastic wrap, heat in
　the microwave for 4 minutes and 30
　seconds, and serve.
■ Choose papaya that is firm and just
　barely ripe for this receipe. Overly ripe
　papaya will become mushy
　when shredded.

6人份
**SERVES 6**

## 西湖牛肉羹

# Western Lake Beef Soup

材料：

| | | | | |
|---|---|---|---|---|
| 牛絞肉 | ··········· 100公克 | | 水 | ··········· 4杯 |
| 熟筍 | ···········35公克 | | 酒 | ··········· 1小匙 |
| 熟洋菇 | ···········25公克 | ② | 塩、味精 | ···各½小匙 |
| 香菜 | ···········少許 | | 胡椒粉 | ·········¼小匙 |
| 蛋白 | ··········· 1個 | | 麻油 | ···········¼小匙 |
| ① | 水 ··········· 2大匙 | ③ | 太白粉 | ····· 1½大匙 |
| | 塩、小蘇打各⅛小匙 | | 水 | ··········· 1½大匙 |

❶牛絞肉入①料醃15分鐘備用。

❷熟筍與香菇均切指甲片（圖1），入②料加蓋加熱5分鐘取出，入牛絞肉快速攪拌（圖2），再加熱1分鐘拌入蛋白及③料即可。

INGREDIENTS:

| | | | |
|---|---|---|---|
| 100g (3½ oz.) | | ground beef | |
| 35g (1¼ oz.) | | cooked bamboo shoots | |
| 25g (1 oz.) | | cooked mushrooms | |
| small bunch | | fresh coriander | |
| 1 | | egg white | |
| ① | 2 T. | water | |
| | ⅛ t. each: | salt, baking soda | |
| ② | 4 c. | water | |
| | 1 t. | rice wine | |
| | ½ t. | salt | |
| | ¼ t. each: | pepper, sesame oil | |
| ③ | 1½ T. each: | cornstarch, water | |

❶ Add ① to the ground beef and marinate 15 minutes.

❷ Cut the cooked bamboo shoots and mushrooms into "fingernail" slices (illus. 1). Add ② , cover, and heat 5 minutes. Remove. Add to the ground beef and mix quickly to combine well (illus. 2). Heat another minute. Mix in the egg white and ③ . Serve.

6人份
**SERVES 6**

# 芋泥牛肉

# Beef With Taro Paste

材料：

| | |
|---|---|
| 芋頭………… 265公克 | |
| 牛里肌肉……… 150公克 | |
| 水………… 2杯 | |
| 蔥花………… 1大匙 | |

① {
蛋白…………½個
水………… 1大匙
醬油………… 1小匙
太白粉……… 1小匙
鹽…………¼小匙
}

② {
豬油…………½大匙
鹽、味精…各¼小匙
}

❶芋頭去皮，切薄片後置盤上，上灑少許水，加蓋加熱 4分30秒，與水同入果汁機中磨碎（圖1），即是芋泥。

❷牛里肌肉切3×3×0.2公分薄片，入①料醃拌備用。

❸芋泥入②料拌勻加熱5分鐘取出，入牛肉拌熟，（圖2）上灑蔥花即可。

INGREDIENTS:

| | | |
|---|---|---|
| 265g (9¼ oz.) | | taro |
| 150g (⅓ lb.) | | lean beef |
| 2 c. | | water |
| 1 T. | | chopped green onion |
| ① | ½ | egg white |
| | 1 T. | water |
| | 1 t. each: | soy sauce, cornstarch |
| | ¼ t. | salt |
| ② | ½ T. | lard |
| | ¼ t. | salt |

❶ Peel the taro, slice thinly, and place the slices on a plate. Sprinkle a little water over the top, cover, and heat 4 minutes, 30 seconds. Place in a blender with the water and puree (illus. 1). This is the taro paste.

❷ Cut the lean beef into 3 x 3 x 0.2cm (1¼″ x 1¼″ x ⅛″) thin slices. Marinate in ①.

❸ Add ② to the taro paste and heat 5 minutes. Remove and add the beef. Stir the beef in the paste until cooked through (illus. 2). Sprinkle chopped green onion over the top and serve.

6人份
**SERVES 6**

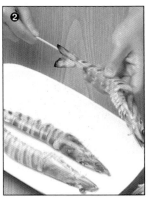

## 忌士焗明蝦

# Shrimp au Gratin

材料：

| | | | |
|---|---|---|---|
| 大明蝦…600公克（約6尾） | 忌士粉…………… 6大匙 |
| 竹籤………………… 6枝 | 牛油……………… 2大匙 |
| | 塩………………… 1小匙 |

❶明蝦去鬚脚及腸泥，洗淨後在腹部切一小刀（圖１）
，並用一枝竹籤（圖２）串直備用。

❷串好的明蝦加１小匙塩，醃約30分鐘備用。

❸烤盤預熱２分鐘，將醃好的明蝦排好，每尾抹上牛
油１小匙，再灑上忌士粉一大匙，加熱７分鐘即可
。

INGREDIENTS:

| | |
|---|---|
| 600g (1⅓ lb.) | jumbo shrimp, unshelled (about 6) |
| 6 | bamboo skewers |
| 6 T. | grated Parmesan cheese |
| 2 T. | butter |
| 1 t. | salt |

❶ Remove the legs and antennae from the shrimp, devein, and wash. Make a small slash in the abdomen of each shrimp (illus. 1), and skewer lengthwise (illus. 2).

❷ Add 1 teaspoon salt to the skewered shrimp and marinate about 30 minutes.

❸ Preheat a baking dish 2 minutes in the microwave. Arrange the marinated shrimp in the dish and spread 1 teaspoon butter on each. Sprinkle 1 tablespoon grated Parmesan cheese over each shrimp, heat in the microwave for 7 minutes, and serve.

6人份
**SERVES 6**

# 韭黃蛤蜊

## Clams with Yellow Chinese Chives

材料：

| | | | | |
|---|---|---|---|---|
| 蛤蜊 | 900公克 | | 酒 | 1小匙 |
| 韭黃 | 250公克 | ① | 塩、糖 | 各½小匙 |
| 油 | 4小匙 | | 味精 | ¼小匙 |
| 蒜末 | 1小匙 | | 胡椒粉 | 少許 |

❶蛤蜊洗淨置盤，蓋上保鮮膜，加熱３分鐘，取出剝下蛤蜊肉（圖１）備用。

❷蒜末加油加熱２分鐘取出備用。

❸韭黃切３公分長段置盤，上放蛤蜊肉（圖２）及①料，並將爆香的蒜末淋在上面，蓋上保鮮膜加熱３分鐘即可。

INGREDIENTS:

| | | |
|---|---|---|
| | 900g (2 lb.) | small clams |
| | 250g (9 oz.) | yellow Chinese chives |
| | 4 t. | cooking oil |
| | 1 t. | minced garlic |
| ① | 1 t. | rice wine |
| | ½ t. each: | salt, sugar |
| | pinch | pepper |

❶ Wash the clams, place in a baking dish, and cover with plastic wrap. Heat in the microwave for 3 minutes. Remove and shuck the clams (illus. 1).

❷ Heat the minced garlic in the oil for 2 minutes.

❸ Cut the yellow Chinese chives into 3cm (1¼'') sections and place in a baking dish. Arrange the clam meat on top of the yellow Chinese chives (illus. 2) and add ①. Pour the fried minced garlic over the top. Cover with plastic wrap and heat for 3 minutes in the microwave. Serve.

6人份
**SERVES 6**

# 涼拌沙拉小卷

## Squid Salad Rolls

### 材料：

| | | | |
|---|---|---|---|
| 透抽 | 235公克 | 火腿絲 | 30公克 |
| 洋芋 | 100公克 | 沙拉醬 | 2大匙 |
| 小黃瓜 | 100公克 | 塩 | ¼小匙 |

❶透抽洗淨，加蓋加熱 2 分30秒，取出待涼備用，洋芋切片上灑少許水，加蓋加熱 5 分鐘取出壓成泥備用。

❷小黃瓜切絲，加¼小匙的塩，略醃，再去汁入洋芋泥、火腿絲及沙拉醬（圖1）拌勻，塞入煮熟的透抽裏（圖2）；塞好後切成寬約0.5公分的圓薄片，即可供食。

### INGREDIENTS:

| | |
|---|---|
| 235g (½ lb.) | fresh squid |
| 100g (3½ oz.) | potatoes |
| 100g (3½ oz.) | gherkin cucumbers |
| 30g (1 oz.) | ham shreds |
| 2 T. | mayonnaise |
| ¼ t. | salt |

❶ Wash the squid thoroughly. Place in a pan, cover, and heat 2 minutes, 30 seconds. Remove and allow to cool. Cut the potatoes into slices and sprinkle a little water over the top. Cover and heat 5 minutes. Remove and mash until smooth.

❷ Shred the gherkin cucumber and sprinkle sprinkle ¼ teaspoon salt over the top. Leave undisturbed for a time, then pour off the liquid that forms. Add the mashed potatoes, ham shreds, and mayonnaise (illus. 1), and mix well. Stuff into the cooked squid (illus. 2). Cut into 0.5 cm (⅓″) rounds and serve.

6 人份
**SERVES 6**

# 鑲百花菇

# Stuffed Chinese Mushrooms

材料：

| | | |
|---|---|---|
| | 小香菇(12朵) | 250公克 |
| | 蝦仁 | 130公克 |
| | 肥肉 | 30公克 |
| ① | 水 | 2大匙 |
| | 油 | ½大匙 |
| | 醬油 | 1½小匙 |
| | 酒 | 1小匙 |
| | 塩、糖 | 各⅛小匙 |
| | 葱段 | 3段 |
| | 薑片 | 2片 |
| ② | 酒 | 1小匙 |
| | 太白粉 | ½小匙 |
| | 麻油 | ¼小匙 |
| | 塩、胡椒粉 | 各⅛小匙 |
| | 蛋白 | 半個 |
| | 薑末 | ½小匙 |
| ③ | 高湯 | ½杯 |
| | 麻油 | ¼大匙 |
| | 醬油 | ¼小匙 |
| | 塩 | ⅛小匙 |
| ④ | 太白粉、水 | 各¾小匙 |

❶香菇泡軟，去蒂(圖１)，加①料入微波爐加熱３分鐘。

❷蝦仁洗淨擦乾，與肥肉一起剁成蝦泥，再調入②料醃10分鐘。

❸將醃好的蝦泥分爲12等份，分別鑲於香菇上(圖２)，上灑少許火腿末及一片香菜葉(圖３)，蓋上保鮮膜加熱２分鐘，取出備用。

❹③料加熱１分30秒，再入④料續熱30秒，取出淋於香菇上即可。

INGREDIENTS:

| | | |
|---|---|---|
| | 12 | small dried Chinese black mushrooms (250g or 9oz.) |
| | 130g (4½ oz.) | shelled shrimp |
| | 30g (1 oz.) | fat pork |
| ① | 2 T. | water |
| | ½ T. | cooking oil |
| | 1½ t. | soy sauce |
| | 1 t. | rice wine |
| | ⅛ t. each: | salt, sugar |
| | 3 1½-sections | green onion |
| | 2 slices | ginger root |
| ② | 1 t. | rice wine |
| | ½ t. | cornstarch |
| | ¼ t. | sesame oil |
| | ⅛ t. each: | salt, pepper |
| | ½ | egg white |
| | ½ t. | minced ginger root |
| ③ | ½ c. | stock |
| | ¼ T. | sesame oil |
| | ¼ t. | soy sauce |
| | ⅛ t. | salt |
| ④ | ¾ t. each: | cornstarch, water |

❶ Soak the dried Chinese black mushrooms until soft. Remove the stems (illus. 1). Mix ① in a baking dish and heat in the microwave 3 minutes.

❷ Wash the shrimp, pat dry, and chop into a paste together with the pork. Mix in ② and allow to marinate 10 minutes.

❸ Divide the shrimp mixture into 12 equal portions. Stuff one portion of the mixture inside each of the 12 mushrooms (illus. 2). Sprinkle a little minced ham and place a fresh coriander leaf on the stuffing surface (illus. 3). Place in a dish, cover with plastic wrap, and heat in the microwave for 2 minutes. Remove and set aside.

❹ Mix ③ together and heat in the microwave 1 minute and 30 seconds. Mix ④ and stir into the mixture just heated, and heat 30 seconds in the microwave. Remove and drizzle over the stuffed mushrooms. Serve.

❶

❷

❸

# 生煎魚排 / Fried Fish Fillet

## 生煎魚排

材料：
魚排（白北魚）…………… ……… 一片（約450公克）
油…………………… 4大匙

① 酒…………… 1大匙
  醬油………… 1小匙
  塩……………½小匙
  糖、胡椒粉………… …………各¼小匙

② 沙拉醬……… 3大匙
  酸黃瓜末…… 1大匙

③ 醬油………… 2大匙
  蒜末………… 1小匙
  糖…………⅛小匙

❶ 魚排洗淨入①料醃30分鐘備用，②、③料分別拌勻備用（圖1）。
❷ 烤盤入油4大匙預熱6分鐘，放入醃好的魚排（圖2）加熱4分鐘，翻面（圖3）續熱4分鐘即可。
❸ 西式吃法可沾拌勻的②料一起食用。中式吃法食用前則將③料淋在魚片上。
■ 這道菜餚若是西餐主食，只供一人食用。

## Fried Fish Fillet

INGREDIENTS:

| | | |
|---|---|---|
| 450g (1 lb.) | | fish fillet (white-fleshed fish) |
| 4 T. | | cooking oil |
| ① | 1 T. | cooking wine |
| | 1 t. | soy sauce |
| | ½ t. | salt |
| | ¼ t. each: | sugar, pepper |
| ② | 3 T. | mayonnaise |
| | 1 T. | minced pickle |
| ③ | 2 T. | soy sauce |
| | 1 t. | minced garlic |
| | ⅛ t. | sugar |

❶ Wash the fish filet and marinate in ① about 30 minutes. Mix ② and/or ③ separately (illus. 1).
❷ Put 4 tablespoons cooking oil in a baking dish and preheat for 6 minutes in the microwave. Place the marinated fish fillet in the dish (illus. 2) and heat for 4 minutes in the microwave. Turn the fish over (illus. 3) and heat another 4 minutes. Serve.
❸ For a Western style meal, serve with ②. For a Chinese meal, pour ③ over the fish.
■ This recipe is a single serving if served as the main dish or in a Western style meal.

# 葱油熗鮮魷 | Squid with Scallions and Oil

材料：

| | | | |
|---|---|---|---|
| 鮮魷魚(淨重)… | 380公克 | 醬油、水… | 各1大匙 |
| 葱絲…………… | 1杯 | 酒………… | ½大匙 |
| 薑絲………… | ¼杯 | ① 太白粉…… | 1小匙 |
| 油…………… | 3大匙 | 塩………… | ¼小匙 |
| | | 胡椒粉……… | 少許 |

❶鮮魷魚洗淨，切交叉花紋(圖1)後切塊(圖2)備用。

❷將切好的魷魚放在蒸盤上，加蓋入微波爐加熱3分30秒取出排盤。

❸油3大匙入微波爐預熱3分鐘，爆香葱、薑絲1分鐘，取出葱薑絲放在魷魚上(圖3)備用。餘油加上①料加熱30秒，再淋在魷魚上即可供食。

INGREDIENTS:

| | |
|---|---|
| 380g (⅘ lb.) | fresh squid (net weight) |
| 1 c. | shedded green onion |
| ¼ c. | shredded ginger root |
| 3 T. | cooking oil |

① 
| | |
|---|---|
| 1 T. each: | soy sauce, water |
| ½ T. | rice wine |
| 1 t. | cornstarch |
| ¼ t. | salt |
| pinch | pepper |

❶ Wash the squid and score in checkerboard fashion (illus. 1), then cut into medium sized pieces (illus. 2).

❷ Place the cut squid on a steaming plate. Cover and heat in the microwave for 3 minutes and 30 seconds. Remove and arrange on a serving platter.

❸ Preheat 3 tablespoons oil for 3 minutes in the microwave, then fry the green onion and ginger root shreds in the oil for 1 minute. Arrange the onion and ginger over the squid (illus. 3). Mix ① into the remaining oil and heat in the microwave for 30 seconds. Drizzle over the squid and serve.

# 豆瓣魚 / Fish with Bean Paste

材料：
吳郭魚… 一尾（700公克）
葱末、油……… 各2大匙

① 酒、醬油…………… 各1½大匙
塩……………½小匙

② 辣豆瓣醬… 1½大匙
薑末、蒜末…………… 各1大匙

③ 水………………½杯
糖、白醋…各½大匙

④ 水…………1大匙
太白粉……1½小匙

❶ 吳郭魚洗淨，入①料醃半小時備用。
❷ 油2大匙入微波爐預熱3分鐘，爆香②料1分30秒後，取出與③料拌勻（圖1），淋在魚上，蓋上保鮮膜加熱9分鐘，取出並將汁液倒在小碗內（圖2）備用。
❸ 蒸魚汁液入④料加熱30秒，取出淋在魚上（圖3），並灑上葱末即可。

## Fish with Bean Paste

INGREDIENTS:

| | |
|---|---|
| 1 whole | porgy (or similar fish; 700g or 1½ lb.) |
| 2 T. each: | minced green onion, cooking oil |
| ① 1½ T. each:<br>½ t. | rice wine, soy sauce<br>salt |
| ② 1½ T.<br>1 T. each: | hot bean paste<br>minced ginger root, minced garlic |
| ③ ½ C.<br>½ T. each: | water<br>sugar, white rice vinegar |
| ④ 1 T.<br>1½ t. | water<br>cornstarch |

❶ Wash the fish and marinate in ① for half an hour. Set aside.
❷ Preheat 2 tablespoons oil in the microwave for 3 minutes, then fry ② in the oil for 1 minute and 30 seconds. Remove and mix in ③ until well blended (illus. 1). Pour over the fish, cover with plastic wrap, and heat in the microwave for 9 minutes. Remove from the oven and pour off the liquid into a small bowl (illus. 2).
❸ Mix the liquid poured off from the fish with ④ until well blended, and heat in the microwave for 30 seconds. Drizzle over the fish (illus. 3) and sprinkle the minced green onion over the top. Serve.

## 生煎蝦餅

材料：

| | | | | |
|---|---|---|---|---|
| 蝦仁 | 150公克 | | 蛋白 | 1個 |
| 肥肉 | 30公克 | | 太白粉 | 1小匙 |
| 葱末 | 2½大匙 | ① | 塩 | ¼小匙 |
| 薑末、洋火腿末 | 各1大匙 | | 味精 | ⅛小匙 |
| 沙拉油 | 2大匙 | | 胡椒粉 | 少許 |
| 黑芝麻、香菜葉 | 各少許 | | | |

❶ 黑芝麻洗淨瀝乾，香菜葉洗淨備用。

❷ 蝦仁去腸泥洗淨，擦乾水份與肥肉剁碎成蝦泥，入葱、薑末並與①料拌勻，用手擠壓成12個圓餅狀（圖1），上面以洋火腿末、黑芝麻及香菜葉點綴（圖2），做成蝦餅。

❸ 烤盤入油2大匙預熱5分鐘後，放入蝦餅（圖3），加熱1分30秒即可取出排盤。

## Fried Shrimp Cakes

INGREDIENTS:

| | |
|---|---|
| 150g (5½ oz.) | shelled shrimp |
| 30g (1 oz.) | fat pork |
| 2½ T. | minced green onion |
| 1 T. | minced ginger root |
| 1 T. | minced ham |
| 2 T. | cooking oil |
| | black sesame seeds, as needed |
| | fresh coriander leaves, as needed |
| ① 1 t. | cornstarch |
| ¼ t. | salt |
| | pepper, as desired |
| 1 | egg white |

❶ Wash the black sesame seeds and drain. Wash the fresh coriander leaves.

❷ Devein the shrimp and rinse clean. Pat away the excess moisture with paper towels. Mince the shrimp with the pork into a fine paste. Add the minced green onion, minced ginger root, and ① until thoroughly combined. Press the shrimp mixture into 12 patties (illus. 1). Sprinkle a little minced ham, some black sesame seeds, and a few coriander leaves onto the top of each patty, pressing them in so that they do not drop off, as a garnish (illus. 2).

❸ Add 2 tablespoons cooking oil to a baking dish and preheat in the microwave for 5 minutes. Arrange the shrimp cakes in the dish (illus. 3) and heat in the microwave for 1 minute and 30 seconds. Arrange on a serving platter and serve.

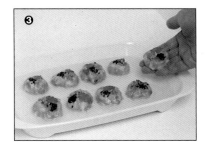

# 豆豉生蠔 / Oysters with Black Beans

材料：

| | | | | | |
|---|---|---|---|---|---|
| 生蠔 | ⋯⋯ 450公克 | | ③ | 醬油⋯⋯⋯ | 2大匙 |
| 油 | ⋯⋯⋯⋯ 2大匙 | | | 糖⋯⋯⋯⋯ | 1小匙 |
| ① | 酒⋯⋯⋯⋯ 2大匙 | | | 酒、麻油⋯各½小匙 | |
| | 塩⋯⋯⋯⋯½小匙 | | | 胡椒粉⋯⋯⅛小匙 | |
| ② | 豆豉、葱末⋯⋯⋯各2大匙 | | | | |
| | 蒜末⋯⋯ 1½大匙 | | | | |
| | 紅辣椒末⋯⋯ 2小匙 | | | | |

❶生蠔洗淨瀝乾，拌入①料，蓋上保鮮膜入微波爐加熱3分鐘取出，瀝乾（圖1），靜置幾分鐘再次瀝乾水份。

❷油2大匙預熱2分鐘，爆香②料1分30秒後入生蠔（圖2）及③料拌勻續熱2分鐘即可。

■1. ②料中的豆豉如爲乾的，必須先用冷水稍微洗淨（圖3）。

2. ③料中的醬油可以醬油膏代替，口味更佳。

3. 此道菜餚應採用小顆生蠔較細嫩鮮美。

## Oysters with Black Beans

INGREDIENTS:

| | | |
|---|---|---|
| | 450g (1 lb.) | fresh oysters |
| | 2 T. | cooking oil |
| ① | 2 T. | rice wine |
| | ½ t. | salt |
| ② | 2 T. each: | Chinese fermented black beans, minced green onion |
| | 1½ T. | minced garlic |
| | 2 t. | minced red chili pepper |
| ③ | 2 T. | soy sauce |
| | 1 t. | sugar |
| | ½ t. each: | rice wine, sesame oil |
| | ⅛ t. | pepper |

❶ Wash and drain the fresh oysters and mix in ①. Cover with plastic wrap and heat in the microwave for 3 minutes. Remove and drain (illus. 1). Allow to sit for a few minutes and drain again.

❷ Preheat 2 tablespoons cooking oil for 2 minutes in the microwave. Fry ② in the oil for 1 minute and 30 seconds. Stir in the oysters (illus. 2) and ③ and heat another 2 minutes. Serve.

■ 1. If using dry Chinese fermented black beans, wash briefly in cold water before using (illus. 3).

2. Thickened soy sauce may be used as a substitute for regular soy sauce for extra flavor.

3. Use small oysters in this recipe for best results.

## 翡翠鮮蛤

材料：
蛤蜊…(約12個) 900公克
絞肉………… 112公克
菠菜…………75公克

① { 水…………… 1小匙
酒……………½小匙
塩、太白粉各¼小匙
麻油…………¼小匙
味精…………少許

❶ 菠菜洗淨置盤上，加蓋加熱 1 分30秒，取出沖涼切碎，水份擠乾入絞肉及①料拌勻成餡。

❷ 大蛤蜊洗淨，加熱 5 分鐘取出，將韌帶割斷（圖 1），取出蛤肉留下一片殼，先放入蛤肉，再放菠菜肉餡並攤平（圖 2），12個全部做好後排盤，加蓋加熱 3 分15秒即可。

## Emerald Clams

INGREDIENTS:

| | | |
|---|---|---|
| 12 | | large clams (900g or 2 lb.) |
| 112g (4 oz.) | | ground pork |
| 75g (2⅔ oz.) | | fresh spinach |
| ① | 1 t. | water |
| | ½ t. | rice wine |
| | ¼ t. each: | salt, cornstarch, sesame oil |

❶ Wash the spinach thoroughly and place on a plate. Cover and heat 1 minute, 30 seconds. Remove, rinse under running water to cool, and chop. Squeeze out excess moisture. Add the ground pork and ① . Mix until well combined to form a filling.

❷ Wash the clams thoroughly and heat 5 minutes. Remove. Cut the tough ligament (illus. 1) and remove the clam meat. Retain one half of the shell. Place the clam meat on the half shell, then stuff with the spinach-ground pork filling until level across (illus. 2). Repeat for the remaining clams and arrange on a plate. Cover and heat 3 minutes, 15 seconds.

# 豆酥鱈魚

Crispy-Topped Cod

材料：

| 鱈魚·············· 430公克 | | 薑酒汁········· 1大匙 |
| 白豆豉··············40公克 | ① | 塩·············· ½小匙 |
| 油·················· 3大匙 | | 味精·········· ¼小匙 |
| 葱花·············· 1大匙 | | 胡椒粉········ ⅛小匙 |
| | | 辣豆瓣醬······ ½小匙 |
| | ② | 糖、麻油···各½小匙 |
| | | 味精·········· ⅛小匙 |

❶ ①料調勻置鱈魚上(圖1)，醃15分鐘入微波爐加蓋加熱5分鐘，取出備用。

❷ 白豆豉剁碎，加油3大匙(圖2)爆香3分30秒，取出入②料拌勻，再置鱈魚上，並灑葱花即可。

INGREDIENTS:

| 430g (15 oz.) | fresh cod |
| 40g (1½ oz.) | light-colored fermented beans |
| 3 T. | cooking oil |
| 1 T. | chopped green onion |
| ① { 1 T. | rice wine with ginger juice |
| ½ t. | salt |
| ⅛ t. | pepper |
| ② ½ t. each: | hot bean paste, sugar, sesame oil |

❶ Mix ① until smooth and sprinkle over the cod (illus. 1). Marinate for 15 minutes. Cover and heat in the microwave for 5 minutes. Remove from microwave.

❷ Mince the light-colored fermented beans, add 3 tablespoons cooking oil (illus. 2), and heat for 3 minutes, 30 seconds in the microwave. Remove from the microwave, add ② , and mix until blended. Sprinkle over the cod, then sprinkle the chopped green onion over the top. Serve.

6人份
**SERVES 6**

## 油爆蝦

材料：

| 劍蝦……300公克（約12尾） | | 蒜末…………… 1大匙 |
| 油………………… 6大匙 | ② | 葱末…………… 1大匙 |
| ① | 酒…………… 1大匙 | | 紅辣椒末…… 1小匙 |
| | 塩…………… ¼小匙 | | 塩………… ¼小匙 |
| | | ③ | 味精………… ⅛小匙 |
| | | | 胡椒粉……… ⅛小匙 |

❶ 劍蝦剪去鬚脚（圖1），除去腸泥並剪開背部（圖2），洗淨後拌入①料醃半小時。

❷ 油4大匙預熱4分鐘，入蝦續熱2分30秒，取出瀝油備用。

❸ 油2大匙預熱2分鐘，爆香②料1分30秒後，隨入③料及蝦並拌勻，續熱1分鐘即可。

■ 如無劍蝦用草蝦代替也可以。

## Garlic Shrimp

INGREDIENTS:

| 300g (⅔ lb.) | fresh medium shrimp, unshelled (about 12) |
| 6 T. | cooking oil |
| ① 1 T. | rice wine |
| ¼ t. | salt |
| ② 1 T. each: | minced garlic, minced green onion |
| 1 t. | minced red chili pepper |
| ③ ¼ t. | salt |
| ⅛ t. | pepper |

❶ Cut the legs and antennae off the shrimp (illus. 1). Devein the shrimp and slit down the back (illus. 2). Wash. Mix in ① and marinate about half an hour.

❷ Preheat 4 tablespoons oil in a baking dish for 4 minutes. Add the shrimp and heat another 2 minutes and 30 seconds. Remove from the baking dish and drain off the oil.

❸ Preheat 2 tablespoons oil for 2 minutes in the microwave. Fry ② in the oil for 1 minute and 30 seconds, then mix in ③ and the shrimp until well blended. Heat another minute and serve.

6人份
**SERVES 6**

# 蛋黃花枝

# Squid With Egg Yolk

材料：
花枝… 600公克（約4隻）
鹹蛋黃………………12個
紫菜………………… 4張

❶花枝去頭、內臟及膜。
❷鹹蛋黃洗淨搓成長條狀，置盤中加熱3分鐘。
❸每3條蛋黃排於紫菜上，連接成長條狀（圖1），塞入花枝肉內（圖2），以牙籤封口，4條均作好，加蓋加熱3分鐘後切小塊排盤。
■用牙籤將封口固定，花枝較不會捲縮。

INGREDIENTS:

| 4 | fresh squid (600g or 1⅓ lb.) |
| 12 | yolks of salt-preserved eggs |
| 4 sheets | purple laver seaweed |

❶ Remove the head, entrails, and outer membrane from the squid.
❷ Wash the salted egg yolks and roll into long cylinder shapes. Arrange on a plate and heat 3 minutes.
❸ Place 3 rolled salted egg yolks on each sheet of purple laver and roll each one up (illus. 1). Stuff one seaweed-egg yolk roll into each of the 4 squid (illus. 2). Secure the ends with toothpicks. Place on a plate, cover, and heat 3 minutes. Cut into small pieces, arrange on a serving plate, and serve.
■ Using toothpicks to secure the ends helps prevent the squid from curling and shrinking.

6人份
**SERVES 6**

## 麻婆豆腐      Szechwan Style Bean Curd

材料：

| | | | |
|---|---|---|---|
| 豆腐·············· 1½塊 | | 水·············· 6大匙 | |
| 絞肉·············70公克 | | 醬油········ 1½大匙 | |
| 葱花·············· 2大匙 | | 酒·············· 1大匙 | ② |
| 花椒粉··········¼小匙 | | 麻油·············· 1大匙 | |
| ① {油·············· 2大匙 葱末·············· 1大匙 辣豆瓣醬······ 1大匙 薑末、蒜末·各1小匙 | | 塩、烏醋···各½小匙 糖············¼小匙 味精··········⅛小匙 | |
| | | ③ {水·············· 3大匙 太白粉········· 1大匙 | |

❶豆腐切1×1×1公分小丁，入鍋備用。

❷爆香①料3分鐘（圖1），入②料及絞肉拌勻，淋於豆腐上（圖2），並加蓋加熱5分熟再入③料，續熱30秒以勾芡、最後取出灑上花椒粉，葱花即可。

INGREDIENTS:

| | | |
|---|---|---|
| 1½ cakes | | bean curd (tofu) |
| 70g (2½ oz.) | | ground pork |
| 2 T. | | chopped green onion |
| ¼ t. | | ground Szechwan pepper (hua chiao) |
| ① | 2 T. | cooking oil |
| | 1 T. each: | minced green onion, hot bean paste |
| | 1 t. each: | minced ginger root, minced garlic |
| ② | 6 T. | water |
| | 1½ T. | soy sauce |
| | 1 T. each: | rice wine, sesame oil |
| | ½ t. each: | salt, Chinese dark vinegar |
| | ¼ t. | sugar |
| ③ | 3 T. | water |
| | 1 T. | cornstarch |

❶ Cut the bean curd into 1cm (⅜″) cubes. Place in a pan.

❷ Fry ① 3 minutes, until fragrant (illus. 1). Mix in ② and the ground pork until well combined, then pour over the top of the bean curd (illus. 2). Cover and heat 5 minutes. Add ③ and heat another 30 seconds to thicken. Remove and sprinkle the ground Szechwan pepper and chopped green onion over the top. Serve.

6人份

**SERVES 6**

## 三色蛋

### Tricolor Egg

材料：

| | | | |
|---|---|---|---|
| 雞蛋 | 3個 | 熱水 | ½杯 |
| 熟鹹蛋 | 2個 ① | 塩 | ¼小匙 |
| 皮蛋 | 2個 | 味精 | ¼小匙 |
| 葱花 | 1大匙 | | |

❶ 熟鹹蛋與皮蛋均先去殼，切小塊，模型舖上保鮮膜（圖1）備用。

❷ 雞蛋打散後，入①料、葱花、鹹蛋及皮蛋拌勻（圖2），倒入模型內，以60%電力煮11分鐘取出，扣於盤上切塊即可。

INGREDIENTS:

| | |
|---|---|
| 3 | fresh eggs |
| 2 | cooked salt-preserved eggs |
| 2 | 1,000-year preserved eggs |
| 1 T. | chopped green onion |
| ① ½ c. | hot water |
| ¼ t. | salt |

❶ Shell the cooked salt-preserved eggs and the 1,000-year preserved eggs and cut into small cubes. Line a baking mold with plastic wrap (illus. 1).

❷ Beat the fresh eggs until smooth, then add ① , the chopped green onion, the cooked salt-preserved egg cubes, and the 1,000-year preserved egg cubes (illus. 2). Pour into the baking mold. Heat at 60% power for 11 minutes, and remove from microwave. Invert onto a plate and cut in squares to serve.

6人份
**SERVES 6**

# 魚子豆腐 / Bean Curd with Fish Roe

材料：

| | | | | |
|---|---|---|---|---|
| 嫩豆腐 | 2塊 | | 水 | ½杯 |
| 魚子 | 120公克 | | 酒 | 1大匙 |
| 青蒜末 | 3大匙 | | 醬油、辣豆瓣醬 | |
| 蒜末 | 1大匙 | ① | 各2小匙 | |
| 油 | 2大匙 | | 糖、麻油 各1小匙 | |
| | | | 塩 ½小匙 | |
| | | | 味精 ⅛小匙 | |
| | | ② | 太白粉、水 各1大匙 | |

❶嫩豆腐切成0.5公分正方塊置盤備用。

❷魚子洗淨去膜（圖1）備用。

❸油2大匙預熱2分鐘，爆香蒜末1分30秒，隨入魚子及①料，並拌勻（圖2）淋在豆腐上（圖3），再加蓋入微波爐加熱5分鐘，最後拌入②料續熱30秒，取出灑上青蒜末即可。

■如果買回來的魚子太腥，可在去膜後用1小匙的酒醃約10分鐘。

■如買不到青蒜末可以葱末代替，但味道差些。

## Bean Curd with Fish Roe

INGREDIENTS:

| | |
|---|---|
| 2 cakes | soft bean curd (tofu) |
| 120g (4 oz.) | fish roe |
| 3 T. | minced garlic sprout |
| 1 T. | minced garlic |
| 2 T. | cooking oil |

| | | |
|---|---|---|
| ① | ½ c. | water |
| | 1 T. | rice wine |
| | 2 t. each: | soy sauce, hot bean paste |
| | 1 t. each: | sugar, sesame oil |
| | ½ t. | salt |
| ② | 1 T. | cornstarch |
| | 1 T. | water |

❶ Cut the bean curd into 0.5cm (¼″) cubes and place in a dish.

❷ Wash the fish roe and remove the outer membrane (illus. 1).

❸ Preheat 2 tablespoons oil in the microwave for 2 minutes, then fry the minced garlic in the oil 1 minute and 30 seconds. Add the fish roe and ① and mix well (illus. 2). Pour over the bean curd (illus. 3), cover, and heat in the microwave 5 minutes. Stir in ② and heat 30 seconds. Sprinkle the minced garlic sprout over the top and serve.

■ 1. If the fish roe has a strong fish odor, soak it in 1 teaspoon rice wine for 10 minutes before using.

2. Minced green onion can be used as a substitute for the minced garlic sprout if unavailable, but the taste will be somewhat different.

## 蝦仁燴豆腐 / Shrimp with Bean Curd

材料：

嫩豆腐（四方型）⋯⋯ 2塊
蝦仁⋯⋯⋯⋯⋯50公克
毛豆⋯⋯⋯⋯⋯40公克
水⋯⋯⋯⋯⋯⋯ 1杯
酒⋯⋯⋯⋯⋯ 1小匙

① { 水⋯⋯⋯⋯⋯¼杯
    塩⋯⋯⋯⋯⋯½小匙
    味精、糖⋯各⅛小匙
    胡椒粉⋯⋯⋯少許

② { 太白粉⋯⋯ 1小匙
    水⋯⋯⋯⋯ 1小匙

❶嫩豆腐切0.5公分四方塊以①料醃10分鐘備用。
❷蝦仁去腸泥洗淨，擦乾水份(圖1)以1小匙 酒醃10 分鐘備用。
❸毛豆加1杯水(圖2)，蓋上保鮮膜加熱4分鐘，取 出洗淨瀝乾備用。
❹將醃好的豆腐加蓋，加熱3分鐘入蝦仁，毛豆（圖 3）加熱2分30秒，最後入②料續熱30秒勾芡即成。

INGREDIENTS:

| | | |
|---|---|---|
| | 2 square cakes | soft bean curd |
| | 50g (1¾ oz.) | shelled shrimp |
| | 40g (1½ oz.) | fresh soybeans |
| | 1 c. | water |
| | 1 t. | rice wine |
| ① | ¼ c. | water |
| | ½ t. | salt |
| | ⅛ t. | sugar |
| | pinch | pepper |
| ② | 1 t. | cornstarch |
| | 1 t. | water |

❶ Cut the bean curd into 0.5cm (¼'') cubes. Marinate in ① 10 minutes.
❷ Devein the shrimp, wash, and dry (illus. 1). Marinate in 1 teaspoon rice wine 10 minutes.
❸ Add 1 cup water to the fresh soybeans or green peas (illus. 2), cover with plastic wrap, and heat 4 minutes in the microwave. Remove, rinse, and drain.
❹ Cover the bean curd and heat 3 minutes in the microwave. Add the shrimp and soybeans (illus. 3), and heat 2 minutes and 30 seconds in the microwave. Add ② and heat 30 seconds to thicken. Serve.

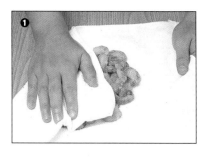

SERVES 6

# 冬菇燒豆腐

# Bean Curd with Chinese Mushrooms

材料：

| | |
|---|---|
| 嫩豆腐 | 2盒 |
| 筍片 | 50公克 |
| 香菇 | 10公克（約6朵） |
| 薑片 | 3片 |
| 蔥 | 6段 |
| 油 | 2大匙 |

① 高湯……………½杯
醬油、蠔油…………
…………各1大匙
糖、塩……各¼小匙
味精…………⅛小匙
② 太白粉、水…各1小匙

❶豆腐切1×2×3公分長方塊備用。
❷香菇泡軟去蒂（圖1）切片備用。
❸油2大匙預熱2分鐘後，爆香香菇、蔥、薑2分30秒（圖2），再入豆腐、筍片及①料並拌勻（圖3）續熱10分鐘，最後入②料加熱30秒勾芡即可。

INGREDIENTS:

| | |
|---|---|
| 2 cakes | soft bean curd |
| 50g (1¾ oz.) | sliced bamboo shoots |
| 10g (⅓ oz.) | small dried Chinese black mushrooms (about 6) |
| 3 slices | ginger root |
| 6 1½''-sections | green onion |
| 2 T. | cooking oil |

① ½ c. — stock
1 T. each — soy sauce, oyster sauce
¼ t. each: — sugar, salt
② 1 t. each: — cornstarch, water

❶ Cut the bean curd into 1×2×3cm (½″ × ¾″ ×1¼″) cubes.
❷ Soak the dried Chinese black mushrooms until soft and remove the stems (illus. 1). Cut into thick strips and set aside.
❸ Preheat 2 tablespoons oil 2 minutes in the microwave. Fry the mushrooms, green onion, and ginger root in the oil for 2 minutes and 30 seconds (illus. 2). Add the bean curd, bamboo shoots, and ①, and combine well (illus. 3). Heat 10 minutes. Stir in ② and heat 30 seconds to thicken. Serve.

# 三鮮百頁捲 / Stuffed Bean Curd Rolls

材料：

| | | | | |
|---|---|---|---|---|
| 百頁 | 6張 | ② | 酒 | 1大匙 |
| 絞肉 | 100公克 | | 葱末 | 1小匙 |
| 蝦仁 | 80公克 | | 塩、麻油 | 各¼小匙 |
| 香菇 | 10公克(約3朶) | | 味精 | 少許 |
| 筍絲 | 40公克 | ③ | 水 | 1杯 |
| ① 水 | 1杯 | | 塩 | ¼小匙 |
| 小蘇打 | 1小匙 | | 味精 | 少許 |
| | | ④ | 水 | 2小匙 |
| | | | 太白粉 | 1小匙 |

❶ 百頁以①料泡10分鐘(圖1)後洗淨備用。香菇泡軟去蒂切絲備用。

❷ 蝦仁去腸泥洗淨，瀝乾水份，切碎加絞肉及②料拌勻成餡，分成6等份備用。

❸ 一張百頁包入一份餡捲成圓筒狀(圖2)，排入深盤中，上置香菇絲、筍絲及③料(圖3)加蓋後加熱8分鐘，取出並將蒸汁倒入碗內拌上④料。

❹ ④料與碗內之蒸汁拌勻，加熱30秒以勾芡，再取出淋在百頁捲上即可。

■ 若買不到百頁可以蛋皮來代替，蛋皮做法如下：

材料：

| | | | | |
|---|---|---|---|---|
| 蛋 | 2個 | ① | 水 | 3大匙 |
| 油 | 2大匙 | | 太白粉 | 1½大匙 |

❶ 蛋打散入①料並拌勻備用。

❷ 平底鍋燒熱入少許油，將①料分六次，煎成6張蛋皮即可。(每次約用2大匙蛋汁、1小匙油)。

## Stuffed Bean Curd Rolls

INGREDIENTS:

| | | |
|---|---|---|
| 6 | | fresh bean curd sheets (pai yeh) |
| 100g (3½ oz.) | | ground pork |
| 80g (3 oz.) | | shelled shrimp |
| 10g (⅓ oz.) | | large dried Chinese black mushrooms (about 3) |
| 40g (1⅓ oz.) | | shredded bamboo shoots |
| ① | 1 c. | water |
| | 1 t. | baking soda |
| ② | 1 T. | rice wine |
| | 1 t. | minced green onion |
| | ¼ t. each: | salt, sesame oil |
| ③ | 1 c. | water |
| | ¼ t. | salt |
| ④ | 2 t. | water |
| | 1 t. | cornstarch |

❶ Soak the fresh bean curd sheets in ① for 10 minutes (illus. 1). Rinse and set aside. Soak the dried Chinese black mushrooms until soft, remove the stems, and cut into julienne strips.

❷ Devein the shrimp, wash, and drain. Chop the shrimp and mix into the ground pork. Add and mix well. This is the filling. Divide into 6 equally sized portions.

❸ Wrap one portion of filling in each of the 6 fresh bean curd sheets, rolling it into a cylindrical shape (illus. 2). Arrange in a deep dish and top with the mushroom and bamboo shoot shreds and ③ (illus. 3). Cover and heat 8 minutes in the microwave. Pour the liquid off into a bowl and mix in ④.

❹ Heat the poured off liquid and ④ 30 seconds to thicken. Drizzle over the top of the bean curd rolls and serve.

■ If fresh bean curd sheets are unavailable, substitute omelette sheets (receipe below).

INGREDIENTS:

| | | |
|---|---|---|
| 2 | | eggs |
| 2 T. | | cooking oil |
| ① | 3 T. | water |
| | 1½ T. | cornstarch |

❶ Beat the eggs until smooth and mix in ①.

❷ Heat a frying pan and add a small amount of oil. Pour some ① in the pan, spreading evenly, and remove when firm. Repeat until you have 6 omelette sheets. (Each sheet requires about 2 tablespoons egg mixture, 1 teaspoon cooking oil.)

# 瑤柱豆腐

材料：

| | | | |
|---|---|---|---|
| 干貝 | 2個(25公克) | ① | 熱干貝汁……¼杯 |
| 蛋 | 2個 | | 沙拉油……⅔大匙 |
| 豆腐 | 2盒 | | 酒……½大匙 |
| 葱花 | 2大匙 | | 太白粉……2小匙 |
| 熱水 | ¾杯 | | 塩……¾小匙 |
| | | | 味精……¼小匙 |
| | | ② | 干貝汁……½杯 |
| | | | 酒……½小匙 |
| | | | 塩、麻油…各¼小匙 |
| | | ③ | 水……1小匙 |
| | | | 太白粉……½小匙 |

❶蛋打散，干貝洗淨加¾杯熱水泡30分鐘，加蓋以70%之電力加熱5分鐘取出，將干貝剝絲(圖1)，湯汁留用。

❷豆腐壓碎(圖2)，入①料、蛋液及干貝絲、並拌勻(圖3)，加蓋以60%之電力加熱14分鐘，取出倒扣於盤上。

❸②料加熱3分鐘取出，入③料續熱30秒勾芡，再取出淋於豆腐上，上灑葱花即可。

# Tofu With Dried Scallops

INGREDIENTS:

| | | |
|---|---|---|
| | 2 | dried scallops (25g or 1 oz.) |
| | 2 | eggs |
| | 2 cakes | bean curd (tofu) |
| | 2 T. | chopped green onion |
| | ¾ c. | hot water |
| ① | ¼ c. | liquid left from soaking dried scallops (hot) |
| | ⅔ T. | cooking oil |
| | ½ T. | rice wine |
| | 2 t. | cornstarch |
| | ¾ t. | salt |
| ② | ½ c. | liquid left from soaking dried scallops |
| | ½ t. | rice wine |
| | ¼ t. each: | salt, sesame oil |
| ③ | 1 t. | water |
| | ½ t. | cornstarch |

❶ Beat the eggs until smooth. Wash the dried scallops and soak 30 minutes in ¾ cup hot water. Cover and heat 5 minutes at 70% power. Remove and tear the scallops into shreds (illus. 1). Retain the liquid.

❷ Mash the bean curd (illus. 2) and mix in ① , the beaten egg, and the scallop shreds until well combined (illus. 3). Cover and heat 14 minutes at 60% power. Remove from microwave and invert onto a plate.

❸ Heat ② 3 minutes and remove. Add ③ and heat another 30 seconds to thicken. Remove and pour over the bean curd mixture. Sprinkle the chopped green onion over the top and serve.

## 干貝雙球

# Vegetable Balls With Dried Scallop

材料：

| | | | | |
|---|---|---|---|---|
| 白蘿蔔 | 600公克 | | 高湯 | 1杯 |
| 胡蘿蔔 | 250公克 | ① | 塩 | ¾小匙 |
| 干貝 | 10公克 | | 味精 | ¼小匙 |
| 熱水 | 1杯 | ② | 水 | 2大匙 |
| 冷水 | ¼杯 | | 太白粉 | 1½大匙 |

❶干貝入熱水 1 杯泡約 1 小時後，加蓋加熱 5 分鐘，取出干貝撕成細絲，湯汁備用。

❷白蘿蔔和胡蘿蔔均去皮 ，再以挖球器挖成圓球狀（圖 1 )。白蘿蔔約240公克，胡蘿蔔約80公克，入水¼杯加蓋加熱10分鐘，續置爐內 3 分鐘，取出再入干貝絲、干貝汁（圖 2 )及①料，續熱 5 分鐘後入②料勾芡即成。

INGREDIENTS:

| | | |
|---|---|---|
| 600g (1⅓ lb.) | | Chinese white radish (daikon) |
| 250g (9 oz.) | | carrot |
| 10g (⅓ oz.) | | dried scallops |
| 1 c. | | hot water |
| ¼ c. | | cold water |
| ① | 1 c. | stock |
| | ¾ t. | salt |
| ② | 2 T. | water |
| | 1½ T. | cornstarch |

❶ Soak the dried scallops in hot water for 1 hour. Cover and heat 5 minutes in the microwave. Remove and tear the scallops into fine shreds. Retain the liquid.

❷ Pare the Chinese white radish and carrots, and cut into balls with a melon baller (illus. 1). Add ¼ cup water to about 240g (8¼ oz.) of the Chinese white radish and 80g (3 oz.) of the carrot, cover, and heat 10 minutes in the microwave. Leave undisturbed in the microwave for 3 minutes after cooking time is completed. Add the scallop shreds, the liquid from soaking the scallops (illus. 2), and ① . Heat 5 minutes, then stir in ② to thicken. 6人份

**SERVES 6**

# 玉蘭芽白

# Cabbage Rolls

材料：

| | |
|---|---|
| 大白菜葉…………………………（6片） | 320公克 |
| 花枝肉………… | 160公克 |
| 肥豬肉…………… | 50公克 |
| ① 高湯…………… | ½杯 |
| ① 塩、味精…各 | ⅛小匙 |
| ① 胡椒粉……… | ⅛小匙 |
| ② 水…………… | ⅔大匙 |
| ② 太白粉……… | ⅔小匙 |
| ③ 蛋白…………… | 1個 |
| ③ 高湯………… | 1大匙 |
| ③ 沙拉油……… | 1小匙 |
| ③ 薑汁、酒…各 | ½小匙 |
| ③ 塩…………… | ½小匙 |
| ③ 太白粉……… | ½小匙 |
| ③ 麻油………… | ½小匙 |
| ③ 味精………… | ⅛小匙 |
| ③ 胡椒粉……… | ⅛小匙 |

❶花枝肉與肥豬肉均剁成泥後入③料拌勻，甩打使有彈性，再分成3等分。

❷大白菜葉加蓋加熱8分鐘後，入冷水中沖涼瀝乾再將兩片白菜葉頭、尾相疊(圖1)，包入1份花枝泥(圖2)捲成長條狀，3條均作好後排入盤中，加熱7分30秒後，切約2公分塊狀，排入盤中。

❸①料加熱1分30秒後入②料續熱30秒取出淋於白菜上即可。

INGREDIENTS:

| | | |
|---|---|---|
| | 6 leaves | Chinese (Nappa) cabbage (320g or 11 oz.) |
| | 160g (5½ oz.) | fresh squid (skinned and cleaned) |
| | 50g (1¾ oz.) | fat pork |
| ① | 1 | egg white |
| ① | 1 T. | stock |
| ① | 1 t. | cooking oil |
| ① | ½ t. each: | ginger juice, rice wine, salt |
| ① | ½ t. each: | cornstarch, sesame oil |
| ① | ⅛ t. | pepper |
| ② | ½ c. | stock |
| ② | ⅛ t. each: | salt, pepper |
| ③ | ⅔ T. | water |
| ③ | ⅔ t. | cornstarch |

❶ Mince the squid and fat pork finely and mix in ①. Throw the mixture against a cutting board several times to increase elasticity. Divide into 3 equal portions.

❷ Place the Chinese cabbage leaves in a baking dish, cover, and heat 8 minutes in the microwave. Cool the leaves in tap water and drain. Stack the cabbage leaves in pairs, with the base of one matched to the upper edge of the other (illus. 1). Place a portion of squid-pork filling in each (illus. 2) and roll into a cylindrical shape. Place the three cabbage rolls in a baking dish and heat 7 minutes, 30 seconds in the microwave. Cut into pieces approximately 2cm (¾") in length. Arrange on a plate.

❸ Heat ② 1 minute, 30 seconds. Add ③ and heat 30 seconds to thicken. Drizzle over the cabbage rolls and serve.

6人份
**SERVES 6**

## 開陽白菜

## Cabbage With Dried Shrimp

材料：

| | | | |
|---|---|---|---|
| 大白菜………… | 600公克 | | |
| 蝦米……………… | 10公克 | | |
| 葱、薑末……… | 各½大匙 | | |
| 油………………… | 2大匙 | | |

① 熱高湯………… 1杯
塩………………… ¾小匙
酒………………… ½大匙
味精……………… ⅛小匙

② 水…………… 3大匙
太白粉……… 1大匙

❶ 大白菜洗淨切塊，葉梗（圖1）加熱7分鐘，再入白菜葉（圖2）續熱4分鐘。
❷ 蝦米泡軟後瀝乾，入葱、薑末及2大匙油加熱2分鐘，再與①料一起拌入白菜再加熱10分鐘，最後以②料勾芡續熱30秒即可。

INGREDIENTS:

| | |
|---|---|
| 600g (1⅓ lb.) | Chinese cabbage (Nappa) |
| 10g (⅓ oz.) | small dried shrimp |
| ½ T. each: | minced green onion, minced ginger root |
| 2 T. | cooking oil |

① 1 c. hot stock
¾ t. salt
½ T. rice wine

② 3 T. water
1 T. cornstarch

❶ Wash the Chinese cabbage and cut into small chunks. Heat the lower stem portion (illus. 1) 7 minutes in the microwave, then add the leafy portion (illus. 2), and heat another 4 minutes.
❷ Soak the small dried shrimp until soft and drain. Add the minced green onion, minced ginger root, and 2 tablespoons cooking oil, and heat 2 minutes. Mix in ① and the cabbage and heat another 10 minutes. Mix in ② and heat another 30 seconds to thicken. Serve.

6人份
**SERVES 6**

# 油燜鮮菇

# Braised Mushrooms

材料：

| 新鮮洋菇········ 300公克 | 水·············· 1杯 |
| 青椒················70公克 | 醬油··········· 1大匙 |
| 油·············· 2大匙 | 糖··········· 1小匙 |
| ① 嫩薑絲········30公克 | ② 塩·············¼小匙 |
| 紅辣椒(切絲)··· 1條 | 胡椒粉、麻油········ |
| | ············各少許 |
| | ③太白粉、水··· 各2小匙 |

❶洋菇洗淨，入②料醃10分鐘。

❷青椒去籽洗淨切與洋菇相等大小之粗塊(圖1)備用。

❸油2大匙預熱2分鐘，爆香①料1分30秒，隨入洋菇及其醃汁，加熱8分鐘，再入青椒(圖2)續熱2分鐘後，隨入③料勾芡加熱30秒即可。

■紅辣椒因品種不同，有些很辣，有些不辣，因此不喜歡辣味者可在切絲時，嘗其辣味，以增減份量。

INGREDIENTS:

| 300g (⅔ lb.) | fresh mushrooms |
| 70g (2½ oz.) | green pepper |
| 2 T. | cooking oil |
| ① { 30g (1 oz.) | shredded young ginger root |
|     1 | red chili pepper, shredded |
| ② { 1 c. | water |
|     1 T. | soy sauce |
|     1 t. | sugar |
|     ¼ t. | salt |
|     pinch | pepper |
|     dash | sesame oil |
| ③ 2 t. each: | cornstarch, water |

❶ Wash the mushrooms and marinate in ② for 10 minutes.

❷ Remove the seeds from the green pepper, wash, and cut into pieces about the same size as the mushrooms (illus. 1).

❸ Preheat 2 tablespoons oil for 2 minutes in the microwave. Fry ① in the oil for 1 minute and 30 seconds. Add the mushrooms with marinade. Heat for 8 minutes in the microwave. Add the green pepper (illus. 2) and heat another 2 minutes. Add ③ and heat for 30 seconds to thicken. Serve.

■ The piquancy of red chili peppers varies greatly. Increase or decrease the amount used according to the "hotness" of the red chili peppers and personal taste.

6人份
**SERVES 6**

# 玉排肉片

# Bitter Melon with Pork and Black Beans

材料：

| | | | |
|---|---|---|---|
| 苦瓜…………… | 400公克 | 水…………… | 3大匙 |
| 里肌肉………… | 120公克 | 蠔油………… | 1小匙 |
| 乾豆豉………… | 1½大匙 | ② 糖………… | ⅔小匙 |
| 蒜末、油……… | 各2小匙 | 塩………… | ¼小匙 |
| 水…………… | 2¼杯 | 味精………… | ⅛小匙 |

① 水…………… 1大匙
醬油、酒… 各1小匙
太白粉……… ½小匙
塩………… ⅛小匙
胡椒粉、麻油……
………各少許

❶ 苦瓜洗淨去籽、去膜，切成1.5×3公分斜段（圖1）
，里肌肉切片入①料醃10分鐘備用。
❷ 冷水2杯入微波爐加熱3分鐘後，入苦瓜段（圖2）
續熱2分鐘，撈出漂涼備用。
❸ 乾豆豉加水¼杯浸泡一下，即取出瀝乾備用。
❹ 油2小匙預熱1分鐘後，爆香蒜末、豆豉（圖3）1
分鐘後，拌入苦瓜、肉片及②料，續熱2分鐘即可。

INGREDIENTS:

| | |
|---|---|
| 400g (14 oz.) | bitter melon |
| 120g (¼ lb.) | lean pork |
| 1½ T. | dry Chinese fermented black beans |
| 2 t. each: | minced garlic, cooking oil |
| 2¼ c. | water |

① 
| | |
|---|---|
| 1 T. | water |
| 1 t. each: | soy sauce, rice wine |
| ½ t. | cornstarch |
| ⅛ t. | salt |
| pinch | pepper |
| dash | sesame oil |

② 
| | |
|---|---|
| 3 T. | water |
| 1 t. | oyster sauce |
| ⅔ t. | sugar |
| ¼ t. | salt |

❶ Wash the bitter melon and remove the seeds and outer membrane. Cut at an angle into 1.5×3cm (⅔''×1¼'')pieces(illus. 1).Cut the pork into slices and marinate in ① for 10 minutes.
❷ Heat 2 cups cold water in the microwave for 3 minutes. Add the bitter melon (illus. 2) and heat another 2 minutes. Remove the melon from the water and place in another bowl of water to cool.
❸ Soak the dry Chinese fermented black beans briefly in ¼ cup of water. Remove from the water and drain.
❹ Preheat 2 teaspoons of oil in the microwave for 1 minute. Fry the minced garlic and black beans in the oil for 1 minute (illus. 3). Stir in the bitter melon, sliced pork, and ②. Heat 2 minutes in the microwave and serve.

# 雙色菜泥

## Two Color Vegetable Puree

材料：

| | | | | |
|---|---|---|---|---|
| 馬鈴薯 | 300公克 | | 奶水 | ¼杯 |
| 菠菜 | 200公克 | ② | 塩 | ¼小匙 |
| 高湯 | ½杯 | | 胡椒粉 | 少許 |

③ 太白粉、水… 各1大匙

①
高湯、奶水…各½杯
塩 ¼小匙
胡椒粉 少許

❶馬鈴薯去皮切成薄片置盤（圖１），蓋上保鮮膜入微波爐加熱８分鐘後，取出趁熱壓成泥狀（圖２），再調入①料拌勻，蓋上保鮮膜後入微波爐加熱３分鐘取出備用。

❷菠菜洗淨切粗段，加高湯½杯入果汁機攪拌後倒在碗中（圖３），入②料拌勻，蓋上保鮮膜加熱３分鐘後，入③料勾芡續熱30秒取出備用。

❸取一大碗，將煮好的❶❷依序倒在湯碗中即可食用（亦可修飾成太極圖形）。

INGREDIENTS:

| | | |
|---|---|---|
| 300g (⅔ lb.) | | potatoes |
| 200g (7 oz.) | | fresh spinach |
| ½ c. | | stock |
| ① | ½ c. each: | stock, milk |
| | ¼ t. | salt |
| | pinch | pepper |
| ② | ¼ c. | milk |
| | ¼ t. | salt |
| | pinch | pepper |
| ③ | 1 T. each: | cornstarch, water |

❶ Peel the potatoes and cut into thin slices. Place in a baking dish (illus. 1), cover with plastic wrap, and heat in the microwave 8 minutes. While still hot, mash the potato slices into a smooth puree (illus. 2). Mix in ① thoroughly. Cover again with plastic wrap and heat in the microwave another 3 minutes.

❷ Wash the spinach thoroughly and chop coarsely. Puree in a blender with ½ cup of soup stock. Pour into a bowl (illus. 3) and mix in ② thoroughly. Cover with plastic wrap and heat in the microwave for 3 minutes. Stir in ③ and heat another 30 seconds to thicken.

❸ Carefully pour the purees prepared in steps ❶ and ❷ separately into a large serving bowl and serve. (The purees can also be made into a Taichi symbol for extra decorative effect.)

# 蠔油鮑魚菇

Abalone Mushrooms with Oyster Sauce

材料：

| | | | |
|---|---|---|---|
| 鮑魚菇 | 300公克 | 高湯 | ½杯 |
| 豌豆夾 | 90公克 | ① 蠔油 | 1½大匙 |
| 蒜末 | 1小匙 | 糖 | ¼小匙 |
| 油 | 1大匙 | 胡椒粉、塩 | |
| 麻油 | ½小匙 | | 各⅛小匙 |
| 水 | 4杯 | ②太白粉、水 | 各2小匙 |
| 紅辣椒 | 1條 | | |

❶鮑魚菇洗淨去蒂切1公分寬之斜片（圖1），放入玻璃碗中加水4杯，加蓋入微波爐加熱10分鐘後，取出瀝乾水份備用。

❷豌豆夾去除旁邊老筋；頭尾切成剪刀狀（圖2）備用。紅辣椒去籽切絲備用。

❸油1大匙與蒜末一起拌勻（圖3），入微波爐爆香50秒後，再入鮑魚菇、豌豆夾、紅椒絲及①料，加熱5分鐘後再拌入②料勾芡續熱30秒，食時趁熱淋上麻油即可。

# Abalone Mushrooms with Oyster Sauce

INGREDIENTS:

| | | |
|---|---|---|
| 300g (⅔ lb.) | | abalone mushrooms |
| 90g (3 oz.) | | Chinese peapods |
| 1 t. | | minced garlic |
| 1 T. | | cooking oil |
| ½ t. | | sesame oil |
| 4 c. | | water |
| 1 | | red chili pepper |
| ① | ½ c. | stock |
| | 1½ T. | oyster sauce |
| | ¼ t. | sugar |
| | ⅛ t. each: | pepper, salt |
| ② | 2 t. each: | cornstarch, water |

❶ Wash the abalone mushrooms and remove the stems. Cut at an angle into 1cm (½'') wide slices (illus. 1). Place in a glass bowl and add the 4 cups of water. Cover and heat in the microwave for 10 minutes. Remove and drain.

❷ Remove the tough strings from the sides of the Chinese peapods while snapping off the two ends. Cut the ends into a wedge shape (illus. 2). Remove the seeds from the red chili pepper and shred.

❸ Mix 1 tablespoon oil with the minced garlic (illus. 3) and fry in the microwave for 50 seconds. Stir in the abalone mushrooms, Chinese peapods, shredded red chili pepper, and ①. Heat for 5 minutes in the microwave. Mix in ② and heat 30 seconds to thicken. Add a few drops of sesame oil and serve hot.

6人份
**SERVES 6**

90

# 白果花菇 | Mushrooms with Gingko Nuts

## 材料：

白果罐頭⋯⋯⋯⋯⋯⋯⋯⋯

⋯⋯⋯⋯ 一罐（180公克）

花菇⋯⋯12朵（約30公克）

油⋯⋯⋯⋯⋯⋯⋯ 1大匙

麻油⋯⋯⋯⋯⋯⋯½小匙

水⋯⋯⋯⋯⋯⋯⋯⋯ 1杯

① { 高湯⋯⋯⋯⋯⋯ 1杯
醬油⋯⋯⋯ 1⅓大匙
塩、糖⋯⋯各¼小匙

② 太白粉、水⋯ 各1小匙

❶花菇泡軟去蒂，每朵切成4份（圖1）備用。

❷白果罐頭去水，再加淨水1杯（圖2），加熱3分鐘
取出洗淨備用。

❸油1大匙預熱2分鐘，爆香花菇2分鐘，入白果及
①料（圖3），拌勻加熱6分鐘，隨入②料勾芡續熱
1分鐘，取出淋上麻油，食前拌勻即可。

■請客時可將煮好的白果、花菇分置腰子盤二端，中
央以小番茄切花分隔開來，較爲美觀。

## INGREDIENTS:

| | |
|---|---|
| 1 can | gingko nuts (290g or ⅔ lb.) |
| 12 | dried Chinese black mushrooms (about 1 oz. or 30g) |
| 1 T. | cooking oil |
| ½ t. | sesame oil |
| 1 c. | water |

① { 
| 1 c. | soup stock |
| 1⅓ T. | soy sauce |
| ¼ t. each. | salt, sugar |

② 1 t. each: cornstarch, water

❶ Soak the mushrooms until soft and remove the stems. Quarter the mushrooms (illus. 1).

❷ Drain the canned gingko nuts (net weight 180g) and add 1 cup of tap water (illus. 2). Heat 3 minutes in the microwave, remove, and rinse under the tap.

❸ Preheat 1 tablespoon oil in the microwave for 2 minutes, then fry the mushroom in the oil for 2 minutes. Add the gingko nuts and ① (illus. 3) and mix thoroughly. Heat 6 minutes in the microwave. Mix in ② and heat another minute to thicken. Sprinkle the sesame oil over the top and mix before serving.

■ For special occasions, place the gingko nuts and mushrooms separately on either side of a divided serving dish. Add a few cut tomato garnishes in the center for a decorative effect.

## 蜜汁胡蘿蔔

## Glazed Carrots

材料：

| 胡蘿蔔 | 300公克 |
|---|---|

① { 水 ‥‥‥‥‥‥ 1杯
  { 塩 ‥‥‥‥‥‥ ¼小匙

② { 新鮮柳丁汁 ‥‥‥ 1杯
  { 蜂蜜 ‥‥‥‥‥ 3大匙
  { 奶油 ‥‥‥‥‥ 1大匙

③ { 太白粉 ‥‥‥ 1½大匙
  { 水 ‥‥‥‥‥‥ 1大匙

❶胡蘿蔔去皮切1公分厚圓片（圖1），入①料後加蓋
入微波爐加熱6分鐘，取出拌入②料（圖2）續熱10
分鐘，再取出拌入③料，加熱1分鐘即可。

INGREDIENTS:

| 300g (⅔ lb.) | | carrots |
|---|---|---|
| ① | 1 c. | water |
| | ¼ t. | salt |
| ② | 1 c. | fresh orange juice |
| | 3 T. | honey |
| | 1 T. | butter |
| ③ | 1½ T. | cornstarch |
| | 1 T. | water |

❶ Peel the carrots and cut into 1cm (⅓″ to
½″) thick rounds (illus. 1). Mix in ① , cover,
and heat in the microwave for 6 minutes.
Remove and mix in ② (illus. 2). Heat 10
minutes in the microwave. Remove and
stir in ③ and heat another minute. Serve.

6人份

# 金茸燴鮑絲

# Golden Mushrooms with Abalone Shreds

材料：

| | | | |
|---|---|---|---|
| 金菇·············· 300公克 | | 水············· 4大匙 | |
| 里肌肉絲、筍絲、鮑魚··· | | 油············· 3大匙 | ② |
| ··················各60公克 | ② | 塩·············½小匙 | |
| ① 水·············· 2大匙 | | 味精、胡椒粉········· | |
| 醬油··········¼小匙 | | ··············各⅛小匙 | |

❶里肌肉絲入①料醃10分鐘備用。

❷鮑魚切3.5公分長絲（圖１）備用。

❸金菇去老根（圖２），洗淨切3.5公分長段 置盤 ，再加入筍絲、鮑魚絲、醃過的里肌肉絲及②料後，蓋上保鮮膜入微波爐加熱５分鐘即可。

INGREDIENTS

| | |
|---|---|
| 300g (⅔ lb.) | golden mushrooms |
| 60g (2 oz.) each: | shredded pork, shredded bamboo shoots, abalone |
| ① { 2 T. | water |
| { ¼ t. | soy sauce |
| ② { 4 T. | water |
| { 3 T. | cooking oil |
| { ½ t. | salt |
| { ⅛ t. | pepper |

❶ Marinate the pork shreds in ① for 10 minutes.

❷ Cut the abalone into 3.5cm (1⅓'') long shreds (illus. 1).

❸ Remove the tough roots from the golden mushrooms (illus. 2), wash, and cut into 3.5cm (1⅓") lengths. Place in a shallow bowl with the bamboo shreds, abalone shreds, marinated pork shreds, and ②. Cover with plastic wrap and heat for 5 minutes in the microwave. Serve.

6人份
**SERVES 6**

## 三絲湯

### Bamboo Shoot and Mushroom Soup

材料：

| | | |
|---|---|---|
| 竹筍⋯⋯⋯⋯⋯ 350公克 | | 水⋯⋯⋯⋯⋯ 5杯 |
| 肉絲⋯⋯⋯⋯⋯75公克 | | 塩⋯⋯⋯⋯⋯¾小匙 |
| 香菇⋯⋯ 15公克（約5朵） | ② | 麻油⋯⋯⋯⋯½小匙 |
| 香菜⋯⋯⋯⋯⋯⋯少許 | | 味精⋯⋯⋯⋯¼小匙 |

| | |
|---|---|
| | 水⋯⋯⋯⋯ 2大匙 |
| | 醬油⋯⋯⋯⋯½小匙 |
| ① | 塩、糖⋯⋯各⅛小匙 |
| | 胡椒粉⋯⋯⋯⋯少許 |

❶肉絲以①料醃10分鐘備用。

❷竹筍去外殼及較老的部分（圖1），其餘部份切細絲，香菇泡軟去蒂切細絲備用。

❸取一大碗入筍絲、香菇及②料，加蓋後加熱10分鐘，再入醃過的肉絲（圖2）續熱2分鐘，食前灑上香菜即可。

INGREDIENTS:

| | | |
|---|---|---|
| 350g (¾ lb.) | | bamboo shoots |
| 75g (2½ oz.) | | shredded pork |
| 15g (½ oz.) | | dried Chinese black mushrooms (about 5) |
| | | fresh coriander, as desired |
| ① | 2 T. | water |
| | ½ t. | soy sauce |
| | ⅛ t. each: | salt, sugar |
| | pinch | pepper |
| ② | 5 c. | water |
| | ¾ t. | salt |
| | ½ t. | sesame oil |

❶ Marinate the shredded pork in ① 10 minutes.

❷ Husk the bamboo shoots and cut away any tough portions (illus. 1). Shred. Soak the dried Chinese black mushrooms until soft, remove the stems, and shred.

❸ Place the shredded bamboo shoots, mushrooms, and ② in a large bowl. Cover and heat 10 minutes in the microwave. Add the marinated shredded pork (illus. 2) and heat another 2 minutes. Sprinkle a little fresh coriander over the top before serving.

6人份
**SERVES 6**

## 原盅三味

## Wintermelon Bowl

材料：

| | | | | |
|---|---|---|---|---|
| 冬瓜 | 180公克 | | 葱 | 2段 |
| 雞腿 | 1隻（250公克） | | 薑片 | 2片 |
| 香菇 | 6朵(12公克) | ① | 熱高湯 | 2杯 |
| 干貝 | 2個(10公克) | | 酒 | 1大匙 |
| 熱水 | 1杯 | | 塩 | 1小匙 |
| | | | 味精 | ½小匙 |
| | | | 胡椒粉 | 少許 |

作法：

❶冬瓜切成3×2×0.5公分片狀（圖1），雞腿剁成2公分立方塊。香菇泡軟去蒂切半（圖2），干貝泡熱水約1小時再撕成細絲，干貝留汁備用。

❷將作法❶所有材料、①料及干貝汁拌勻後加蓋加熱15分鐘即可。

INGREDIENTS:

| | | |
|---|---|---|
| 180g (6½ oz.) | | wintermelon |
| 1 | | chicken leg (250g or 9 oz.) |
| 6 | | dried Chinese black mushrooms (12g or ⅖ oz.) |
| 2 | | dried scallops (10g or ⅓ oz.) |
| 1 c. | | hot water |
| ① | 2 sections | green onion |
| | 2 slices | ginger root |
| | 2 c. | hot stock |
| | 1 T. | rice wine |
| | 1 t. | salt |
| | pinch | pepper |

❶ Cut the wintermelon into 3 x 2 x 0.5cm (1¼″ x ¾″ x ⅛″) slices (illus. 1). Cut the chicken leg into 2cm (¾″) cubes. Soak the mushrooms until soft, remove the stems, and cut each in half (illus. 2). Soak the dried scallops in hot water about 1 hour, then tear into fine shreds. Retain the soak water from the dried scallops.

❷ Mix all the ingredients in step ❶ together with ① and the soak water from the scallops. Cover and heat 15 minutes. Serve.

6人份
**SERVES 6**

# 海鮮生蠔湯 / Oyster Potage

## 材料：

| | | | |
|---|---|---|---|
| 生蠔 | 300公克 | ③太白粉、水… | 各3大匙 |
| 嫩豆腐 | 一塊 | 薑(切絲) | 5片 |
| 油條(切碎) | 一條 | 葱花 | 1大匙 |
| ①酒、太白粉… | 各1小匙 | ④香菜末 | 1大匙 |
| ②熱高湯 | 6杯 | 胡椒粉 | ¼小匙 |
| 塩 | 1¾小匙 | 麻油 | ¼小匙 |
| 味精 | ¼小匙 | | |

❶生蠔用清水輕輕漂洗乾淨(圖1)，瀝乾水份，加①料入微波爐加熱2分鐘取出，瀝乾(圖2)備用。

❷嫩豆腐切約0.6公分正方塊小丁，入②料及生蠔(圖3)，加蓋後入微波爐加熱3分鐘，隨入③料拌勻續熱30秒，取出灑上④料，上桌前再灑上油條即成。

■1. 喜歡胡椒香味者，可多加一些胡椒粉。

　2. 如果②料中的高湯是涼的，就必須多加熱3分鐘。

## INGREDIENTS:

| | | |
|---|---|---|
| 300g (⅔ lb.) | | fresh oysters |
| 1 cake | | soft bean curd |
| 1 | | Chinese fried cruller (yu-tiao), chopped |
| ① | 1 t. each: | rice wine, cornstarch |
| ② | 6 c. | hot soup stock |
| | 1¾ t. | salt |
| ③ | 3 T. each: | cornstarch, water |
| ④ | 5 slices | ginger root, shredded |
| | 1 T. each: | chopped green onion, minced fresh coriander |
| | ¼ t. each: | pepper, sesame oil |

❶ Gently wash the fresh oysters in water (illus. 1) and drain. Add ① and heat 2 minutes in the microwave. Drain (illus. 2).

❷ Cut the bean curd into 0.6cm (⅓'') cubes. Stir in ② and the oysters (illus. 3). Cover and heat 3 minutes in the microwave. Mix in ③ and heat 30 seconds. Sprinkle ④ over the top. Sprinkle some chopped Chinese fried cruller over the top before serving.

■ 1. The amount of pepper used may be increased, if desired.

　2. If the stock used in ② is not hot, add 3 minutes to the cooking time.

# 雞絨玉米湯 / Chicken and Corn Soup

## 材料：

| | | |
|---|---|---|
| 雞胸肉 | 50公克 | |
| 玉米醬 | 1罐 | |
| 雞蛋 | 2個 | |
| 火腿末 | 1大匙 | |
| 黑胡椒粉 | 少許 | |

① 
- 水 …… 3大匙
- 太白粉 …… 1小匙
- 酒 …… ½小匙
- 塩 …… ¼小匙
- 味精 …… ⅛小匙

② 
- 水 …… 4杯
- 塩 …… ¼小匙
- 味精 …… ⅛小匙

③ 
- 水 …… 1大匙
- 太白粉 …… 2小匙

❶雞胸肉剁成雞絨（圖1），入①料拌勻（圖2），醃約10分鐘，雞蛋打散備用。

❷玉米醬入②料，加蓋入微波爐加熱8分鐘後隨入雞絨、蛋液及③料，迅速攪拌均勻（圖3），再入微波爐加熱2分鐘，取出即可。

❸食用時灑上火腿末及黑胡椒粉。

■若將②料中的水改用高湯，味道更鮮美。

## INGREDIENTS:

| | | |
|---|---|---|
| 50g (1⅔ oz.) | chicken breast meat | |
| 1 can | cream style corn | |
| 2 | eggs | |
| 1 T. | minced ham | |
| pinch | pepper | |

① 
- 3 T. water
- 1 t. cornstarch
- ½ t. rice wine
- ¼ t. salt

② 
- 4 c. water
- ¼ t. salt

③ 
- 1 T. water
- 2 t. cornstarch

❶ Mince the chicken finely (illus. 1), mix in ① (illus. 2), and marinate 10 minutes. Beat the eggs.

❷ Add ② to the cream style corn, cover, and heat 8 minutes in the microwave. Add the minced chicken, beaten egg, and ③, and beat quickly until smooth (illus. 3). Heat 2 minutes in the microwave.

❸ Sprinkle some minced ham and black pepper over the top before serving.

■ Using soup stock for the water in ② will add extra flavor to this soup.

6人份
**SERVES 6**

# 菠菜豆腐湯

# Spinach and Bean Curd Soup

材料：

| | | | | | |
|---|---|---|---|---|---|
| 嫩豆腐················ 2塊 | | | 高湯·············· 5杯 | |
| 筍··············· 100公克 | | | 塩·············· 1小匙 | |
| 菠菜············· 100公克 | | ② | 麻油·········· ½小匙 | |
| 瘦肉片············40公克 | | | 味精·········· ⅛小匙 | |
| ① | 水············· 2大匙 | | 胡椒粉··········少許 | |
| | 醬油··········½小匙 | | ③太白粉、水··· 各 3大匙 | |
| | 塩············¼小匙 | | | |

❶ 嫩豆腐切約0.5公分正方塊，筍切0.5公分片狀（圖1），菠菜洗淨切碎（圖2）備用。

❷ 瘦肉片入①料醃10分鐘備用。

❸ 將豆腐、筍片及②料放入大碗內，加蓋後加熱8分鐘，再入肉片及菠菜（圖3），續熱4分鐘，最後入③料加熱勾芡30秒即可。

■ 瘦肉片用已去筋之里肌肉，肉質較嫩。

INGREDIENTS:

| | | |
|---|---|---|
| 2 cakes | | soft bean curd |
| 100g (3½ oz.) | | bamboo shoots |
| 100g (3½ oz.) | | fresh spinach |
| 40g (1⅓ oz.) | | pork, sliced |
| ① | 2 T. | water |
| | ½ t. | soy sauce |
| | ¼ t. | salt |
| ② | 5 c. | stock |
| | 1 t. | salt |
| | ½ t. | sesame oil |
| | pinch | pepper |
| ③ 3 T. each: | | cornstarch, water |

❶ Cut the soft bean curd into 0.5cm (¼'') cubes, and the bamboo shoots into 0.5cm (¼'') thick slices (illus. 1). Wash the spinach thoroughly and chop (illus. 2).

❷ Marinate the pork slices in ① 10 minutes.

❸ Place the bean curd, bamboo shoots, and ② into a large bowl, cover, and heat 8 minutes in the microwave. Add the pork slices and spinach (illus. 3) and heat another 4 minutes. Add ③ and heat 30 seconds to thicken. Serve.

■ Use lean pork with the sinews removed for best results.

# 蘿蔔排骨湯      Pork and Radish Soup

材料：

| 小排骨 | 220公克 | | 水 | 6杯 |
|---|---|---|---|---|
| 白蘿蔔 | 270公克 | | 薑 | 6片 |
| 紅蘿蔔 | 130公克 | ① | 塩 | 1¼小匙 |
| 香菜 | 少許 | | 味精 | 少許 |

❶小排骨剁小塊(圖1)，加熱2分鐘去血水，取出洗淨備用。

❷紅、白蘿蔔去皮切與小排骨同等大小的滾刀塊（圖2），香菜洗淨備用。

❸小排骨、紅白蘿蔔及①料同置容器內（圖3），加蓋加熱50分鐘，取出灑上香菜即可。

INGREDIENTS:

| 220g (½ lb.) | pork ribs |
|---|---|
| 270g (9½ oz.) | Chinese white radish (daikon) |
| 130g (4½ oz.) | carrot |
| | fresh coriander, as desired |

| | | |
|---|---|---|
| | 6 c. | water |
| ① | 6 silces | ginger root |
| | 1¼ t. | salt |

❶ Chop the pork ribs into small chunks (illus. 1; or have your butcher do it for you). Heat 2 minutes in the microwave and wash to remove the bloody liquid.

❷ Peel the carrot and Chinese white radish and roll-cut into chunks about the same size as the pork rib chunks (illus. 2). Wash the fresh coriander.

❸ Place the pork rib chunks, carrot, Chinese white radish, and ① in a container (illus. 3), cover, and heat 50 mInutes in the microwave. Garnish with fresh coriander and serve.

# 黃魚丸湯 | Fish Ball Soup

## 材料：

| | |
|---|---|
| 黃魚……1尾（約600公克） | |
| 青江菜………… 200公克 | |
| 肥肉………………40公克 | |

② 熱水…………… 6杯
　 塩…………… 1小匙

③ 芹菜末……… ½大匙
　 黑胡椒………¼小匙

① 芹菜末…… 1½大匙
　 薑末………… ½大匙
　 蛋白…………… ½個
　 塩…………… ⅜小匙
　 味精、胡椒粉………
　 …………… 各⅛小匙

❶黃魚洗淨去骨、去皮、取淨肉（圖1），淨重約180公克，備用。

❷魚肉及肥肉一起剁成泥（圖2），再與①料拌勻（圖3），甩打至有彈性，做成18個魚丸備用。

❸青江菜洗淨，大棵的切成4份，小棵的對切，備用。

❹將②料放入大碗內預熱2分鐘，隨入魚丸及青江菜，加蓋後加熱6分鐘，取出灑上③料即可。

■黃魚丸做好後放入冰箱冷藏10～20分鐘較佳。

## INGREDIENTS:

| | |
|---|---|
| 1 whole | Chinese yellow croaker (or other white-fleshed fish; about 600g or 1⅓ lb.) |
| 200g (7 oz.) | ching kang tsai (or other leafy green) |
| 40g (1⅓ oz.) | fat pork |

① 1½ T. — minced celery, preferably Chinese
　 ½ T. — minced ginger root
　 ½ — egg white
　 ⅜ t. — salt
　 ⅛ t. — pepper

② 6 c. — hot water
　 1 t. — salt

③ ½ T. — minced celery, preferably Chinese
　 ¼ t. — black pepper

❶ Wash, skin, and bone the fish. You should have about 180g (6½ oz.) of fish meat, net weight (illus. 1).

❷ Mince the fish together with the fat pork (illus. 2). Mix in ① (illus. 3), and throw the paste against a counter or cutting board until springy in texture. Make into 18 equally sized balls.

❸ Wash the greens. If using large bunches, quarter lengthwise; if small, halve lengthwise.

❹ Place ② in a large bowl and preheat 2 minutes in a microwave. Add the fish balls and greens, cover, and heat 6 minutes in the microwave. Sprinkle on ③ and serve.

■ After forming the fish balls, allow to cool and become firm in the refrigerator for 10 to 20 minutes for better results.

## 蘿蔔絲蛤蜊湯

## White Radish and Clam Soup

材料：

| 白蘿蔔絲……… 150公克 | | 熱水…………… 4杯 |
| 蛤蜊……12個(約150公克) | ① | 塩…………… 1小匙 |
| 薑絲………………10公克 | | 味精、酒…各½小匙 |
| 葱花……………… 2大匙 | | 白胡椒粉………少許 |

❶ 蛤蜊吐砂(圖1)後洗淨。

❷ ①料入蛤蜊、白蘿蔔絲、薑絲(圖2)，後加熱6分鐘，取出灑上葱花及白胡椒粉即可。

INGREDIENTS:

| 150g (⅓ lb.) | | shredded Chinese white radish (daikon) |
| 12 | | clams (about 150g or ⅓ lb.) |
| 10g (⅓ oz.) | | shredded ginger root |
| 2 T. | | chopped green onion |
| | 4 c. | hot water |
| ① | 1 t. | salt |
| | ½ t. | rice wine |
| pinch | | white pepper |

❶ Soak the clams in cold water so that they expel the sand they contain (illus. 1). Wash thoroughly.

❷ Add the clams, shredded Chinese white radish, and shredded ginger root to ① (illus. 2). Heat 6 minutes. Remove from microwave and sprinkle the chopped green onion and white pepper over the top. Serve.

6人份
**SERVES 6**

# 蒜子雞湯

# Chicken Soup with Garlic

材料：

雞半隻或雞腿２隻⋯⋯⋯⋯

⋯⋯⋯⋯⋯⋯⋯ 600公克

蒜仁⋯⋯⋯⋯⋯⋯75公克

油、葱末⋯⋯⋯ 各1大匙

① ｛水⋯⋯⋯⋯⋯⋯ 6杯

醬油、塩⋯ 各1小匙

❶雞洗淨去多餘的肥油後剁成小塊（圖１），置盤加熱３分鐘取出，再洗淨瀝乾以便除去血水，備用。

❷油１大匙預熱２分鐘，爆香蒜仁２分鐘（圖２），隨入雞塊及①料，加蓋加熱15分鐘，取出灑上葱末即可。

■1. 喜歡大蒜味道者，可多加15公克的蒜仁。

2. 這道湯的蒜仁入口即化。

INGREDIENTS:

½                      chicken or 2 chicken legs (600g or 1⅓ lb.)

75g (2½ oz.)         peeled garlic

1 T. each:            cooking oil, minced green onion

① ｛6 c.              water

1 t. each:           soy sauce, salt

❶ Wash the chicken, remove excess fat, and chop the chicken into chunks (illus. 1). Place in a dish and heat 3 minutes in the microwave. Wash and drain to remove the bloody liquid. Set aside.

❷ Preheat 1 tablespoon oil 2 minutes in the microwave, then fry the garlic in the oil for 2 minutes (illus. 2). Add the chicken and ①, cover, and heat 15 minutes. Sprinkle the minced green onion over the top and serve.

■ 1. An extra 15g (½ oz.) peeled garlic may be added if desired.

2. The garlic in this soup literally melts in the mouth.

6人份
**SERVES 6**

## 枸杞燉雞

Chicken Stewed with Wolfberry Seeds

材料：

| | |
|---|---|
| 雞腿⋯⋯ 2隻（470公克） | ① ｛熱水⋯⋯⋯⋯⋯ 5杯 |
| 枸杞⋯⋯⋯（圖1）30公克 | ｛酒⋯⋯⋯⋯⋯⋯ 4大匙 |

❶枸杞洗淨備用；雞腿剁小塊（圖2）加熱 3 分30秒，
　取出洗淨瀝乾水份。

❷雞腿、枸杞與①料放入大碗內加蓋加熱15分鐘即可。

■ 可依個人喜好調整熱水及酒之比率。

INGREDIENTS:

| | |
|---|---|
| 2 | chicken legs (470g or 1 lb, ½ oz.) |
| 30g (1 oz.) | wolfberry seeds (kou-ch'i-tzu; illus. 1) |
| ① ｛5 c. | hot water |
| ｛4 T. | rice wine |

❶ Wash the wolfberry seeds thoroughly.
Chop the chicken legs into small chunks
(illus. 2), and heat 3 minutes, 30 seconds.
Remove, rinse clean, and drain.

❷ Place the chicken, wolfberry seeds, and
① in a large bowl. Cover, heat 15 minutes, and serve.

■ The proportions of water and rice wine
may be adjusted according to individual
taste.

6人份
**SERVES 6**

# 桂圓糯米粥

## Sweet Rice Congee with Dried Longans

材料：

| | | | |
|---|---|---|---|
| 圓糯米 | 150公克 | ① ｛ 熱水 | 1杯 |
| 桂圓乾 | 40公克 | 酒 | 1大匙 |
| 熱水 | 6杯 | 糖 | ½杯 |

❶桂圓乾加①料備用。

❷圓糯米洗淨，加熱水6杯，入微波爐加熱12分，再以50%電力加熱6分鐘，入桂圓（圖1），續以50%電力加熱7分鐘取出，拌入½杯糖（圖2）即可。

INGREDIENTS

| | |
|---|---|
| 150g (⅓ lb.) | glutinous (mochi; sweet) rice |
| 40g (1½ oz.) | dried longans |
| 6 c. | hot water |
| ① ｛ 1 c. | hot water |
| 1 T. | rice wine |
| ½ c. | sugar |

❶ Add ① to the dried longans.

❷ Wash the glutinous rice and add 6 cups hot water. Heat 12 minutes in the microwave. Heat another 6 minutes at 50% power. Add the dried longans (illus. 1). Heat another 7 minutes at 50% power. Stir in ½ cup sugar (illus. 2). Serve.

6人份
**SERVES 6**

# 油　飯

# Savory Sticky Rice

材料：

| 長糯米 | 300公克 |
|---|---|
| 絞肉 | 75公克 |
| 紅葱頭末 | 37公克 |
| 香菇絲 | 10公克 |
| 蝦米 | 2大匙 |
| 油 | 4大匙 |
| 水 | 1杯 |

① 
| 醬油 | 3大匙 |
|---|---|
| 麻油 | 1大匙 |
| 味精 | ½大匙 |
| 塩、胡椒粉各 | ¼大匙 |

❶ 蝦米泡軟瀝乾備用，長糯米洗淨泡水約半日，瀝乾後入冷水1杯，加熱10分鐘續以30%電力加熱6分鐘，在爐內放置5分鐘，再取出。

❷ 油4大匙與紅葱頭末拌勻（圖1），加熱8分鐘半，入絞肉、香菇絲、蝦米（圖2），加熱3分鐘再入①料與糯米飯拌勻，續熱3分鐘即可。

INGREDIENTS:

| 300g (⅔ lb.) | long-grain glutinous rice |
|---|---|
| 75g (2½ oz.) | ground pork |
| 37g (1½ oz.) | minced shallots |
| 10g (⅓ oz.) | dried Chinese black mushrooms, soaked till soft and julienned |
| 2 T. | small dried shrimp |
| 4 T. | cooking oil |
| 1 C. | water |

① 
| 3 T. | soy sauce |
|---|---|
| 1 T. | sesame oil |
| ¼ T. each: | salt, pepper |

❶ Soak the dried shrimp until soft and drain. Soak the long-grained glutinous rice about half a day. Drain and add 1 cup cold water. Heat 10 minutes at full power, then another 6 minutes at 30% power. Leave undisturbed in the microwave for 5 minutes after cooking time is completed. Remove.

❷ Mix the 4 tablespoons cooking oil with the minced shallots (illus. 1). Heat 8 minutes, 30 seconds. Add the ground pork, the mushroom strips, and the shrimp (illus. 2). Heat 3 minutes and add ① . Stir into the cooked glutinous rice until well combined and heat 3 minutes. Serve.

6人份
**SERVES 6**

110

# 蘿蔔糕

材料：

| 再來米 | 300公克 | | 塩 | ½小匙 |
| 白蘿蔔 | 600公克 | ① | 味精 | ½小匙 |
| 水 | 1½杯 | | | |

❶容器內舖上玻璃紙（圖1），備用。
❷米浸泡過夜，瀝乾加水入果汁機打碎。
❸白蘿蔔切粗塊入果汁機打碎，加熱12分取出，趁熱
　加入米漿（圖2）及①料拌勻，再放入容器內加熱15
　分，取出待涼即可。

# Radish Cake

INGREDIENTS:

| 300g (⅔ lb.) | long-grain rice |
| 600g (1⅓ lb.) | Chinese white radishes (daikon) |
| 1½ c. | water |
| ① ½ t. | salt |

❶ Line a baking dish with cellophane (illus. 1).
❷ Soak the rice overnight. Drain and pulverize in a blender.
❸ Cut the Chinese white radish into chunks and grate in a blender. Heat 12 minutes in the microwave. Add to the pulverized rice while still hot (illus. 2), then mix in ① until well blended. Pour into the cellophane-lined dish and heat 15 minutes in the microwave. Allow to cool and serve.

6人份
**SERVES 6**

## 杏仁豆腐

## Almond Tofu

材料：

| | |
|---|---|
| 開水 | 3杯 |
| 洋菜 | 7公克 |
| 糖 | 3大匙 |
| 鳳梨片罐頭 | 1罐 |
| 櫻桃 | 少許 |

① { 鮮奶 …… 1杯
    杏仁露 …… 4½大匙 }

❶開水入洋菜（圖1）及糖，加熱5分鐘，再以50%電力加熱18分鐘後過濾（圖2），入①料拌勻，待冷却凝固切成菱形小塊。

❷鳳梨片取出切小塊與罐內糖水、杏仁塊及櫻桃混合即可。

INGREDIENTS:

| | |
|---|---|
| 3 c. | water |
| 7g (¼ oz.) | agar-agar |
| 3 T. | sugar |
| 1 can | pineapple chunks |
| a few | maraschino cherries |

① { 1 c.  milk
    2 T.  almond extract }

❶ Add the agar-agar (illus. 1) and sugar to the water. Heat 5 minutes at full power, then another 18 minutes at 50% power. Strain (illus. 2). Mix in ① thoroughly and refrigerate until firm. Cut into diamond shapes.

❷ Mix the pineapple chunks with the syrup from the can, the almond tofu diamonds, and the cherries. Serve.

## 紙杯蛋糕

## Cupcakes

材料：

奶水‧‧‧‧‧‧‧‧‧‧‧‧‧‧‧40公克 ② { 糖粉‧‧‧‧‧‧‧‧ 150公克

蛋‧‧‧‧‧‧‧ 4個（250公克） ② { 奶油‧‧‧‧‧‧‧‧ 100公克

① { 低筋麵粉‧‧‧ 300公克 { 酥油‧‧‧‧‧‧‧‧‧‧‧50公克

① { 發粉‧‧‧‧‧‧‧‧‧ ½小匙

❶①料過篩備用。

❷②料打至發白，將蛋分４次加入並拌勻，再入過篩後之①料，輕輕攪拌均勻，續入奶水拌勻，最後裝入擠花袋中（圖１）。

❸蛋糕模型，舖上紙杯模，再將麵糊擠入紙杯模，每個約裝二分之一滿（圖２），每六個蛋糕一組，入微波爐中加熱２分30秒即可。

■冷却後之蛋糕因奶油成份多，會較硬，食用前可在表面噴上少許水份以20秒鐘加熱即可回軟。

INGREDIENTS:

| | | |
|---|---|---|
| 40g (1½ oz.) | | milk |
| 4 | | eggs (250g or 8¾ oz.) |
| ① | 300g (⅔ lb.) | low-gluten (or cake) flour |
| | ½ t. | baking powder |
| ② | 150g (⅓ lb.) | sugar |
| | 100g (3½ oz.) | butter |
| | 50g (1¾ oz.) | shortening |

❶ Sift ①.

❷ Cream ② until fluffy. Add the eggs, one at a time, mixing well between each one. Add ① and mix gently until smooth. Add the milk and mix until blended. Transfer to a pastry bag (illus. 1).

❸ Arrange the paper cupcake cups in a muffin mold. Squeeze batter into each cup until about half full (illus. 2). Bake 6 at a time in the microwave for 2 minutes, 30 seconds. Serve.

■ Because of their high butter content, the cupcakes will become somewhat hard after cooling. Spray a little water over the top of the cupcakes and heat 20 seconds in the microwave to soften.

6人份
**SERVES 6**

# 炸餛飩

材料：

絞肉……………110公克
餛飩皮………………24張
炸油……………… $2\frac{1}{2}$杯

①
- 蛋白…………… $\frac{1}{4}$個
- 葱末……… $1\frac{1}{2}$小匙
- 薑末………… 1小匙
- 塩…………… $\frac{3}{8}$小匙
- 味精、酒、麻油……
  ……………各$\frac{1}{4}$小匙
- 胡椒粉……… $\frac{1}{8}$小匙

②
- 醬油………… 1大匙
- 黑醋、辣油…………
  ……………各$\frac{1}{2}$小匙

❶絞肉入①料拌匀成內餡，分成24等份備用。
❷每張餛飩皮包入１份餡，即成餛飩。
❸深盤內入炸油２$\frac{1}{2}$杯(圖１)，加蓋預熱７分鐘後，入12個餛飩(圖２)，加熱２分30秒，即可撈起，並以吸油紙瀝乾去油(圖３)。
❹原油再加熱２分鐘，入剩餘的12個餛飩，續熱２分30秒後，撈起再以吸油紙瀝乾油份即可。
❺將②料拌匀作爲炸好餛飩的沾汁。
■ ②料中的醬油若改用醬油露，則味道更佳。

# Fried Wontons

INGREDIENTS:

| | |
|---|---|
| 110g ($\frac{1}{4}$ lb.) | ground pork |
| 24 | wonton skins |
| $2\frac{1}{2}$ c. | oil for deep frying |
| ① $\frac{1}{4}$ | egg white |
| $1\frac{1}{2}$ t. | minced green onion |
| 1 t. | minced ginger root |
| $\frac{3}{8}$ t. | salt |
| $\frac{1}{4}$ t. each: | rice wine<br>sesame oil |
| $\frac{1}{8}$ t. | pepper |
| ② 1 T. | soy sauce |
| $\frac{1}{2}$ t. each: | Chinese dark vinegar,<br>chili oil |

❶ Mix ① into the ground pork for the filling. Divide into 24 equal portions.
❷ Wrap one portion of the meat filling in each of the wonton skins.
❸ Add $2\frac{1}{2}$ cups cooking oil to a deep baking dish (illus. 1). Cover and preheat in the microwave for 7 minutes. Place 12 of the wontons in the oil (illus. 2). Heat in the microwave for 2 minutes and 30 seconds. Remove the wontons from the oil and drain on absorbent paper (illus. 3).
❹ Heat the remaining oil another 2 minutes in the microwave. Place the 12 remaining wontons in the oil and heat for 2 minutes and 30 seconds. Remove the wontons from the oil and drain on absorbent paper.
❺ Mix ② until well blended and serve with the fried wontons as a dip.

❶
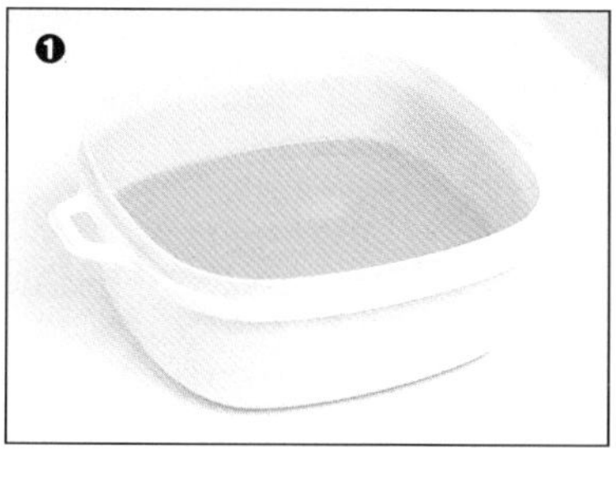

❷

❸

# 八寶粥 / Eight Jewel Congee

材料：

| | | | |
|---|---|---|---|
| 紅豆 | ……¼杯 | 紅棗 | ……12粒 |
| 綠豆 | ……¼杯 | 桂圓肉 | ……40公克 |
| 白米 | ……½杯 | ① 水 | ……1½杯 |
| 去皮花生仁 | ……½杯 | 小蘇打 | ……⅛小匙 |
| 小米 | ……¼杯 | ② 糖 | ……1杯 |
| 水 | ……6杯 | 葡萄乾 | ……3大匙 |

❶紅豆、綠豆及白米洗淨後加水2杯泡4小時（圖1）
備用。

❷花生仁加①料，加蓋後入微波爐加熱15分鐘，取出
洗淨（圖2）備用。

❸小米、紅棗均洗淨備用。

❹將泡好的❶料加入❸料、桂圓肉、花生仁及剩餘的
4杯水，加蓋後入微波爐（圖3），以80％的電力加
熱30分鐘，取出加②料並拌勻，待糖溶化後即可食
用。

## Eight Jewel Congee

INGREDIENTS:

| | |
|---|---|
| ¼ c. | red (adzuki) beans (dry) |
| ¼ c. | mung beans (dry) |
| ½ c. | white rice |
| ½ c. | blanched raw peanuts |
| ¼ c. | millet |
| 6 c. | water |
| 12 | Chinese red dates (jujubes) |
| 40g (1⅓ oz.) | dried longans |
| ① 1½ c. | water |
| ⅛ t. | baking soda |
| ② 1 c. | sugar |
| 3 T. | raisins |

❶ Wash the red beans, mung beans, and rice. Soak in 2 cups of water for 4 hours (illus. 1).

❷ Add ① to the peanuts, cover, and heat 15 minutes in the microwave. Drain and rinse the peanuts (illus. 2).

❸ Wash the millet and Chinese red dates.

❹ To the ingredients from step ❶ add those from step ❸, the dried longans, peanuts, and the remaining 4 cups of water. Cover and heat in the microwave (illus. 3) for 30 minutes at 80% power. Add ② and mix until blended. Serve after the sugar is completely dissolved.

# 玉米煎餅

材料：

雞蛋‥‥‥‥‥‥‥ 2個
白細糖‥‥‥‥‥‥ 1大匙
玉米醬‥‥‥‥‥‥半杯

① { 低筋麵粉‥‥‥‥半杯
    酸粉‥‥‥‥‥½小匙

蜂蜜或果醬‥‥‥‥適量

❶將①料過篩備用。將雞蛋的蛋黃與蛋白分開，蛋白
加白細糖，用直型打蛋器打至硬性發泡，再依序加
入蛋黃、過篩後之①料及玉米醬，以橡皮刮刀攪拌
均勻(圖1)。

❷烤盤預熱3分30秒後，用湯匙將麵糊一大匙、一大
匙的放在烤盤上(圖2)，每盤放4大匙，加熱45秒
，翻面(圖3)續熱45秒，即可取出。

❸第二次、第三次烤餅時，烤盤只須預熱1分30秒，
其餘步驟與第一盤相同，三次共烤12片。

❹食用時可淋上蜂蜜或果醬。

# Corn Fritters

INGREDIENTS:

| 2 | eggs |
|---|---|
| 1 T. | sugar |
| ½ c. | cream-style corn |
| ① { ½ c. | low-gluten or cake flour |
|     ½ t. | baking powder |
| | honey or jam, as desired |

❶ Sift ① together. Separate the eggs. Add the sugar to the egg whites and beat until stiff. Add, in the following order, the egg yolks, ①, and the cream-style corn, and mix with a spatula until well blended (illus. 1).

❷ Preheat a baking sheet or pan for 3 minutes and 30 seconds in the microwave. Drop 4 tablespoonsful of the batter, separately, onto the baking sheet (illus. 2). Heat for 45 seconds in the microwave. Turn the fritters over (illus. 3) and heat another 45 seconds. Remove.

❸ For the second and third batches, the baking sheet need be preheated only 1 minute and 30 seconds; then follow the same procedure as for the first batch. Yield will be 12 fritters made in 3 batches.

❹ The fritters may be served with honey or jam, if desired.

❶

❷

❸

# 水果蛋糕

## Fruit Cocktail Cake

材料：

| | | | |
|---|---|---|---|
| 高筋麵粉 | 1杯 | 奶油(溶化) | ¾杯 |
| 椰子粉 | 1杯 | 雞蛋 | 3個 |
| 白細糖 | 1½杯 | 奶水 | ½杯 |
| 酸粉 | 2小匙 | 什錦水果(顆粒狀) | 2杯 |
| 核桃(壓碎) | 1½杯 | | |

❶麵粉過篩，與糖、椰子粉及酸粉拌勻備用。

❷奶水、蛋及奶油先拌勻(圖1)，再入❶料(圖2)一起拌勻，最後加入什錦水果及核桃(圖3)並拌勻成麵糊備用。

❸模型內抹上奶油再灑上少許麵粉，倒入麵糊，再入微波爐，加熱14分鐘即可。

INGREDIENTS:

| | |
|---|---|
| 1 c. | high-gluten or all-purpose flour |
| 1 c. | desiccated (or flaked) coconut |
| 1½ c. | sugar |
| 2 t. | baking powder |
| 1½ c. | chopped walnuts |
| ¾ c. | melted butter |
| 3 | eggs |
| ½ c. | milk |
| 2 c. | fruit cocktail, drained |

❶ Sift the flour and mix together with the sugar, coconut, and baking powder.

❷ Mix the milk, egg, and butter (illus. 1). Stir in the dry ingredients from step ❶ (illus. 2) until thoroughly blended. Finally, fold in the drained fruit cocktail and chopped walnuts (illus. 3).

❸ Grease and flour a cake pan, then pour in the batter. Bake in the microwave for 14 minutes. Serve.

# 創造和樂的社會

──是我們的理想

本著"取之於社會‧用之於社會"的理想‧味全文化教育基金會自民國68年成立以來‧即不斷地致力於**培育專門人才**，促進家庭和諧，致力國際交流，**創造安和社會**，功效卓益‧受到社會大眾一致的肯定與尊敬。

以行動實踐服務社會的熱誠‧每年舉辦兒童冬夏令營‧家庭系列專題講座、全國金廚獎烹飪比賽、紅毯之旅、童詩童畫比賽等社會公益活動。

## 味全文化教育基金會
**WEI-CAUAN CULTURAL AND EDUCATIONAL FOUNDATION**

地址：台北市松江路125號5F
電話：(02)5084331　(02)5063564
ADDRESS: 5TH FL, 125, SUN-CHIANG RD,
　　　　　TAIPEI, TAIWAN, R.O.C.
TEL: (02)5084331　(02)5063564

# 爲生活增添趣味
## ——————使家庭更幸福美滿

美好的日子是需要去創造的，味全家政班以"增進生活情趣，提昇精神層次"的理念，致力於傳遞各種技藝，提供各類常識，使生活更豐富活潑，使家庭更幸福美滿。

- 烹飪班：中國菜、西餐、日本料理、中點、西點、餐盤裝飾等⋯。
- 插花班：西洋花、池坊流、小原流。
- 美姿班：瑜伽、韻律、有氧舞蹈。
- 語文班：英語、日語、西班牙文。
- 兒童才藝班：
  繪畫、電腦、心算、書法、英語、作文、課業輔導、韻律、中國結、紙黏土、剪紙⋯⋯等。

## 味全文教基金會附設家政班
**WEI-CAUAN CULTURAL AND EDUCATIONAL FOUNDATION**

地址：台北市松江路125號5F
電話：(02)5084331　(02)5063564
ADDRESS: 5TH FL, 125, SUN-CHIANG RD,
　　　　　TAIPEI, TAIWAN, R.O.C.
TEL: (02)5084331　(02)5063564

味全

# 從容自信的每一天

因爲準備好了「味全冷凍調理食品」，妳也可以像她一樣，做個掌理生活，游刃有餘的現代婦女。

生活中，我常要輪番扮演著女兒、太太、媽媽、職業婦女……的不同角色，就是再忙，也不願意隨便打發家人的胃口；平常，我都是準備「味全冷凍調理食品」，因爲我小孩愛吃的水餃、雲吞、包子、燒賣……味全都有，連對吃最挑剔的老公，也讚不絕口，說有親手作的味道……。

## 現代人的新主食───
# 味全冷凍調理食品

最重要的是，「味全冷凍調理食品」一上市就獲得了「優良冷凍食品標誌」的肯定，品質當然無話可說。

從容的安排每一天的生活
自信的做個稱職的現代婦女，請
爲家人準備───現代人的新主食

鮮肉雲吞　鮮肉包　豬肉水餃　燒賣　貢丸

---

# 味全冷凍調理食品

味全消費者服務中心　　TEL：080- 221007

想要追求精緻的口味感受？ 開

就有

## 味全冷凍調理食品

您看到的這一桌豐富美味的大餐，全都是味全以冷凍調理食品為您料理的哦！味全冷調是由味全家政班以獨家研究的配方精心調製即使最挑剔的嘴，也會讚不絕口，再加上口味繁多，不論您想吃什麼，只有味全冷凍調理食品最能滿足您追求多樣美味的需求，選擇味全，相信您會滿意。

味全冷凍調理食品均榮獲CAS優良冷凍食品双標誌。

味全消費者服務中心電話：080-221007

豬肉水餃　　韭菜水餃　　素食水餃　　斤裝貢丸　　鮮肉包　　炸雞塊　　鮮肉雲吞　　菜肉雲吞

給您100分的烹調享受

# 有人說它是味精；有人說它不太像是味精

## 味全高鮮味精
### 小小一匙卻兼具了
### 海帶香菇柴魚的高度鮮味
### 因此才備受矚目

● 新一代的調味品
● 日本武田技術合作
● 素食可用

除非您親自試一試
這個備受矚目的話題才能夠得到真正的解答

味全消費者服務專線：(080)221007